For years stories of c
ure to build the King
but, that's how thing
never happen.' Finally a book describing that it not only can happen but is happening right here in our home and native land.

TIM SCHROEDER, Teaching Pastor
Trinity Baptist, Kelowna, B.C.

These are real stories from real churches that bring to life the journey of taking risks, even some crazy ones. Moving to the un-comfortable is the critical step in finding authentic mission en-gagement. Its confirmation that Canadian churches are catching up with what God is doing. And the questions at the conclusion of each story make this more than an interesting read—they challenge and encourage anyone who wants to follow Jesus. I believe everyone can learn something from this book.

DAVE TOYCEN, President and CEO
World Vision Canada

Going Missional will provide some helpful signposts to Christ-followers across the country who are asking, "What is God call-ing us to be and do? What do we need to take with us on the next step of the journey of response, and what do we need to leave behind?"

AILEEN VAN GINKEL, Vice-President, Ministry Services,
The Evangelical Fellowship of Canada

We've been reading about missional theory for some time, much of it coming from thinkers outside of the Canadian context. Now *Going Missional* offers us real-life stories of Canadian churches who have embraced missional practice. The power of these stories is in their capacity to inspire the rest of us to think creatively about how to engage our communities with the impact and implications of the gospel. The thirteen churches described in the book did not set out to lead the nation, but wouldn't it be wonderful if they did!

KENTON C. ANDERSON, Director of the Centre
for Ministry Excellence of Trinity Western
University, Dean of Northwest Baptist Seminary,
and Author of *Choosing to Preach*.

Imagine the impact if your church was truly more missional in your city or town. Such a dream can happen! For church leaders open to new ideas and willing to take some risks, *Going Missional* can help you envision fresh ways of blessing those outside the walls of your church.

JERRY REDDY, Senior Pastor,
Hillside Baptist Church, Moncton, N.B.

Stiller and Metzger bring a wealth of experience, in congregations, in development, and in journalism to this work. It's a lively read! But the book also provides vivid pictures of what a more holistic kind of mission looks like on the ground. As an Anglican I could not help but feel that they were rediscovering what the old idea of the "parish," a place within which Christians are called to minister to all the inhabitants, was about. I recommend this book enthusiastically as a way to put flesh and bones on the missional idea.

GEORGE SUMNER, Principal and Helliwell
Professor World Mission, Wycliff College,
University of Toronto

Here's a must read for those who desire to join Christ's example of meeting people's needs, showering them with love in their community and marketplace.

ROSEMARY FLAATEN, M.A. Speaker
Author of *A Woman and Her Relationships*

Karen Stiller and Willard Metzger have done the churches of Canada a great service. This book elbows us squarely in the ribs, then dares tempt us with the reasonable hope that God can use the likes of us in a sweeping renewal across this nation.

PHIL CALLAWAY, Speaker and
Best-Selling Author of *Laughing Matters*

Our church has become really good at fundraising and cutting cheques. But we really want to grow in sharing the love, life and hope of Christ in our own community. The problem is: we feel stuck... what should we do? How can we help? Karen Stiller shared her research for this book with our own outreach and mission team as she worked on it. We incorporated some of the new ideas right away, and we are on the brink of changing how we do outreach and mission because of it.

CATHY COOPER, Head of Outreach and Mission,
Church of the Ascension, Port Perry, Ont.

Going Missional is not about a new fad in the church but a return to our roots. "For God so loved the world..." that He came on a mission; and as His body, it's our mission too. Profiling 13 churches across Canada, this book offers a way of relief for a Church that's stuffed with itself. Written with humility and openness, *Going Missional* is encouraging because it doesn't prescribe a formula, but rather invites the reader to lift their sail and catch "the wind of God." It describes, in profoundly practical ways, big and small steps that less than perfect churches have taken to move in a missional direction. *Going Missional* not only makes you think; it gives you hope.

DOUGLAS MOTT, Senior Pastor, First Congregational Church of Halifax, Chair of Jesus to the Nations Missions Conference

If you've ever sat in church and found yourself thinking "there has to be more to the Christian life than this," *Going Missional* is for you. This important book documents the struggles and achievements of 13 Canadian churches striving to listen for where God is at work in their communities, and then joining in. It is an honest, yet inspiring book - best read meditatively - in order to ponder its lessons and insights and to ask the Spirit how you might apply them. God *is* at work in Canada, in sometimes surprising ways and places. And as we seek to be His Church rather than our own, He will allow us the privilege and joy of being used in His Kingdom work of bringing about justice, and making wrong things right.

PATRICIA PADDEY, Producer, Listen Up TV

Karen Stiller always wields a delightfully poignant pen. *Going Missional* weaves together a bright tapestry of diverse experiences. Having some familiarity with a number of the represented churches, I found in this book a compelling, illuminating and inspiring series of vignettes, deftly stitched together with thoughtful narrative. May it help us all in our sojourn.

REV. JAMIE MCINTOSH, Executive Director, International Justice Mission Canada

GOINGMISSION🍁L

Conversations with 13 Canadian Churches Who Have Embraced Missional Life

KAREN STILLER
and Willard Metzger

GOING MISSIONAL
Conversations with 13 Canadian Churches Who Have Embraced Missional Life

Scripture taken from the Holy Bible, New International Version. Copyright © 1973, 1978, 1984 International Bible Society. Used by permission of Zondervan Bible Publishers.

ISBN-13: 978-1-77069-021-9

Printed in Canada.

Published by Word Alive Press
131 Cordite Road, Winnipeg, MB R3W 1S1
www.wordalivepress.ca

WORD ALIVE PRESS
Just Write!

To Brent, Erik, Holly and Thomas,
the best story I have ever been a part of.
—K.S.

To Lois and Patrick,
for pushing me to the starting line.
—W.M.

TABLE OF CONTENTS

FOREWORD

At the Willow Creek Association's annual Leadership Summit a few years ago, Jim Collins challenged church leaders to ask themselves this question; "Would it make any noticeable difference in your community if your church ceased to exist?"

In other words, were their churches living out their faith in such a way that people's lives were impacted and genuine needs were being met? The term that has come to embody this movement is "Going Missional."

⋏   ⋏   ⋏

At The Leadership Centre Willow Creek Canada, we have had a front-row seat observing churches across our country fully embrace what it means to be on a mission, and we have constantly sought ways to re-tell these stories to inspire other leaders who are guiding their churches through a missional transition.

Through the process of collecting these stories, we were reminded yet again just how powerfully God is at work in and through His church across Canada. And we began to wonder just what might happen if these stories which we have assembled were to inspire hundreds—or even thousands—of church leaders to leverage their leadership gifts in guiding their churches towards missional living.

When our friends at World Vision Canada shared a similar passion, it did not take long for us to start dreaming of ways we might collaborate to share these stories with as many people as possible. The result is the book you are now holding in your hands, *Going Missional: Conversations with 13 Canadian Churches Who Have Embraced Missional Life*.

Read these stories carefully. Read them prayerfully. Allow them to inspire you to lead your congregation towards being fully "on mission". We believe the result can change leaders, churches and entire communities.

The next time you are asked, "Would it make any noticeable difference in your community if your church ceased to exist?", our prayer is that the answer will be, "Yes, it would make all the difference in the world!"

—SCOTT COCHRANE
Executive Director, The Leadership Centre
Willow Creek Canada

INTRODUCTION

Increasingly, we are looking for inspiration that we can relate to, that is authentic. Inspiration that gives churches hope to build from who we are and from where we are at right now.

This is precisely the beauty of the missional church concept. Missional celebrates the exemplary within the ordinary. God is active in every community, every household across the country. To be missional is to tap into the common experience of God's activity. God is *already* active—and calling the Church to get into the action.

We are happy to report, that, increasingly it seems, the Canadian Church is responding.

Going Missional: Conversations with 13 Canadian Churches who Have Embraced Missional Life tells the stories of 13 churches— of various sizes, denominations and locations—who are entering into their own communities in deep and meaningful ways. For some, the shift from inward to outward has shaken them to their core. Others have taken huge risks. Some have taken small steps on this journey. Some have never forgotten God's call to be incarnate right where they are. Some are remembering it anew.

In the process of selecting the churches to be profiled, we searched for diversity of experience, activities, challenges and locations. The good news is that there are many, many Canadian churches that could have easily found their place in a book like this. We were happy that it was so difficult to choose.

In these pages, you will discover a small sampling of missional character and activity, not an exhaustive definition of it—simply because that would be impossible. And we hope that churches separated by geography and denomination may discover a common ground in vision and mission as they read about each other.

We also hope that readers will be relieved to find a truly Canadian book telling the stories of churches that represent our distinctly Canadian experience. Missional activity is a growing Canadian church experience that has touched countless churches, and even the lives and work of the writers.

As a freelance writer for 15 years, Karen Stiller has told many stories of churches and people engaged in transformative ministry across the country. Her work as a journalist, along with her life as a minister's spouse, has afforded her a unique perspective on the joys and struggles of going missional.

Willard Metzger's experience with the missional church has spanned over a decade of leadership within the

Mennonite Church of Canada, one of the first national church bodies to intentionally restructure themselves around a missional church paradigm.

In recent years, the concept of the "missional church" and its associated language/theories have reshaped expectations and modes of operation within the Canadian church across most denominations. In its most basic form, the missional church concept is to discern the activity of God and then to align with that activity.

The task of the Church is not to first discern a vision and purpose and then to obtain God's blessing and anointing, which is what many of us have done for many years. It is instead to discover what God is *already* doing and then to get on board with that activity.

This basic missional understanding has some potentially unsettling assumptions:

- God is active outside of the Church.
- God has not been waiting for the Church before initiating redemptive activity.
- And therefore, God's activity is not limited to the definitions and parameters often assumed by the Church.

Once our vision is broadened, this new awareness of God's activity becomes explosive and beautiful. It is our prayer that this book will spur fresh reflection, discussion and inspiration. God is at work. And Canadian churches are joining in.

CHAPTER ONE
Friends

New Life Church
_____

Duncan, B.C.
www.newlifechurch.bc.ca

AVERAGE WEEKLY ATTENDANCE: 650-700

DENOMINATIONAL AFFILIATION: Canadian Baptists of
    Western Canada

YEAR FOUNDED: 1983

Missional activity is often viewed through the lens of how the Church can influence others towards a greater experience of God. But the flip side is also an important missional characteristic—the Church expressing new openness to how a deeper experience of God itself can occur.

Often, the journey towards missional awareness begins with the assumption that the primary position of the Church is as a divine in-

strument for healing, restoration and wholeness. The Church is indeed the primary vessel for expressing God's grace and mercy. God's invitation for experiencing healing and wholeness is heard best and most clearly through the Church. However, God also desires to draw the Church into a deeper understanding and experience of that same healing. As a result, humility and confession may become an important part of the missional vehicle.

As a pastor, I admit that sometimes my dreams of outreach effectiveness were coloured by my need to be seen as a leader of a growing, and therefore successful, church. Growth is not an ignoble cause. But growth was often as much about my own image as it was about seeing the image of God realized in the hearts of others.

Success for the Church is measured by how well it reflects the character of God and cooperates with the activity of God. A church can grow and attract people, but it may not necessarily be missional. A missional church is prepared to risk its own image to restore the image of God and align itself with God's redemptive activity, no matter what the cost.

—W.M.

⅄   ⅄   ⅄

The Cowichan Valley on Vancouver Island is one of those places that you wander through and think, that if only you could live here, you'd finally buy that cherry-red kayak you've contemplated for years. It is beautiful.

About 74,000 people call it home, including members of the Cowichan Tribes, the largest First Nation Band in British Columbia, whose roots extend back into that particularly lush ground about 4,500 years. Roughly half of the tribe's members live on the Reserve, while others make their homes in one of the many communities that dot the valley, including Duncan.

Duncan tops the list of quintessentially Canadian towns for two reasons. First, it is home to the world's largest hockey stick and puck, measuring an impressive 205 feet and weighing 61,000 pounds. Secondly, like many Canadian towns built on and around First Nation lands, the area has a history of segregation, rancour, suspicion and racism that has run deeply, quietly and both ways between First Nations people and much of the rest of the community.

Historically, the Canadian Church has not exactly been the balm of Gilead. The shame of residential schools and their abuses has been well researched, carefully documented, publicly condemned and—finally—apologized for by key denominations. But that controversial history is still a millstone around the Church's neck as it tries to reach out to First Nations people to share faith, make amends, or even just to make friends.

Making friends is where it all began for New Life Community Church in Duncan, a Baptist congregation of about 700 or so and growing. Pastor and author Mark Buchanan says he was always concerned about First Nations issues, in a "remote, distant 'I wish somebody would do something about that kind-of-way.'"

Then, they *did* do something about it. And it could serve as a template for missional-living, loving and co-abiding for other churches that recognize there is something amiss in their relationship with the Aboriginal people they share community with.

It was big news for the Cowichan Tribes when they were awarded the privilege of hosting the 2008 North American Indigenous Games, an Aboriginal Olympics that brings together thousands of athletes, cultural participants and eager onlookers from across North America to compete in events like archery, badminton, baseball, and canoeing, among a long list of others.

Rick Brant, a Mohawk, was CEO of the Indigenous Games and moved from Ontario to the Cowichan Valley to head up the event. Rick checked out New Life as a possible church home for his family on the very Sunday the church held their first meeting about how they could support the Games.

"The church was a key driver in the community in terms of recognizing the Games as a primary vehicle for reconciliation with the First Nations people," says Rick. "They spearheaded a community-wide awareness campaign that dovetailed nicely with our own efforts. The strength of the work was the understanding that, if we want to stand with them, we have to understand them. A relationship doesn't start with someone knocking on your door and explaining the gospel, when there is such a history of distrust."

Mark Buchanan and his team recognized that the Indigenous Games was a ready-made opportunity to serve the Aboriginal community by providing help for the Games itself. Organizers needed 3000 volunteers for everything from handing out water bottles after a sweaty lacrosse tournament to setting up booths for the Artist Market where crafters would display their wares for the 10 days of the Games.

The timing of the Games and the opportunity they represented coincided perfectly with New Life's growing consciousness that they could build a bridge across the very noticeable gap between the different communities in the Cowichan Valley.

"About five years ago, it hit me with force that we needed to do something," says Mark. "We began dreaming and scheming. We realized, as we boned up on the history of the First Nations people in our neck of the woods, that there had been such a series of gross injustices committed that we needed to come in a spirit of repentance and humility, not with a 'here we are, lucky you!' stance. We knew we had a lot to learn."

So, Mark and Graham Bruce, one of his New Life partners in the business of dreaming and scheming, created a workshop called "Understanding the Nations" which they offered to churches in the Cowichan Valley in the months leading up to the Indigenous Games.

"What really interested me about the Games," says Graham, a former politician who still retains a strong passion for public life, "was the opportunity to build friendship. I thought that it could be inspired reconciliation, the Games being the vehicle. With 10,000 people coming, we needed all kinds of volunteers, but we had to be careful so as to not come across the wrong way."

The workshop was an in-your-face kind of experience that demystified key elements of Cowichan history, culture and spirituality.

"There is an innocent ignorance out there, and there's also a deeper feeling that there's been a wrong and we don't know how to go about correcting it. Then, there's the feeling of 'my life's pretty good, why do I want to look over there, and besides, they just have their hand out.' They don't actually, but that's the perception," says Graham. "There was a 10-foot wall running through our community. A chief told me that, even in his 40s standing in line at a bank, he felt inferior."

The "Understanding the Nations" workshops allowed participants to admit that they harboured those negative perceptions. That is a very intimidating thing for many people to do—and perhaps especially for Christians who often prefer to disguise their occasional nasty side, especially when they are at a seminar with other Christians.

"We used humour," reveals Graham. "During our Question-and-Answer session, I would ask the *Archie Bunker*-style questions. I acted like the white bigot so I could ask the stupid questions and make the racist comments. We used examples that everybody could take to their own heart."

This attempt to speak honestly was long overdue, according to Graham. "There can be an 'over-sympathy' and 'over-sensitivity' where you don't talk honestly with each other. You're so afraid of saying the wrong thing that it becomes platitudes. There's a continuation of mistrust because people don't speak honestly," says Graham.

One of the workshop helpers was Jenn George. Her mother is Caucasian, "a European mutt," and her father is Cowichan. Jenn grew up in a middle-class family, attended a private school, lived on the Reserve and worshipped at New Life.

"The workshops weren't patronizing—they were about understanding. They weren't about white people being so bad, but that the church should be the ones to make an effort, not just to bring native people to church, but to really understand why things are the way they are," explains Jenn.

It's one thing, says Jenn, to look at a Reserve and criticize—"Look at how they live, look at the Third World conditions"—but it's quite another thing to examine why. The workshops dealt head-on with the residential school issue and educated participants about what life was like before the schools, during, and of course, after.

"The idea of the forum was to go into the churches and bring it home to people what it would have been like to have your children taken from you and how that would have impacted the rest of your life. In a very short period of time, life changed dramatically to despair and hopelessness," explains Graham. "We have a 'get over it!' mentality. There is a necessity to deal with some of this history, not to maintain a victim type of present, but so you can communicate with others to understand what they have been through. And then move on."

The "moving on" included an outpouring of volunteers for the games, not only from New Life, but others from the Church community.

"It was amazing to see how God was able to use the work we were doing, that passion. To reach out to the Cowichan and say 'We are going to support you in this,'" says Jenn. "It wasn't 'Hey brother, I know you've been hurt but I have Jesus.' A lot of relationships began, and it's continued."

About 1,000 Christians attended the workshops, and municipal government employees attended a version crafted especially for them.

During the process, it occurred to Graham Bruce and his wife that learning someone's language is a great sign of respect and honour. "If you went off to Hawaii, there are words you would already know. We asked ourselves how we could honour that language, which is honouring the people, and get people to learn some words."

They printed up 5,000 buttons that said "Huy ch 'qa, which means "thank you" in Cowichan, and distributed them to business owners, merchants and volunteers for the games.

"It was, in itself, quite amazing the reaction people had. I don't know why they were so surprised because in any other part of the world, if you make an attempt to learn a language, barriers come down," says Graham.

Part of the success was being genuine and keeping it simple. "Often, we look for these great huge things to do, but sometimes, it is the small gestures that are huge. New Life had really become a leader in the community in the reconciliation that was happening. Other churches came along too. The greater Christian community really stepped up to it."

Graham says: "The Church, as a hierarchy, often gets caught up in 'We can't go in there without the right protocols.'" says Graham. "And I would say 'We're just making friends here. Let's not get too hung up on this. We don't need a license to go in and make friends.'"

As a result, New Life has become a very large church in the community, says Graham. "By our presence, we've moved back into the public square. It doesn't mean we have to go running down the street singing hallelujah. It's doing quiet work. People know they can ask us for help now."

And that does happen. Aware of New Life's presence and willingness to help, community groups are increasingly accessing it. The legacy of the Indigenous Games continues in other events like a Walk of the Nations, an annual community festival that begins with a walk from one end of Duncan to another, crossing the tracks—literally—to get to the other side.

"We wanted people to say, 'Yes, we can walk together and support each other.' There is an openness now in the community that wasn't there before," says Jenn, who is one of the organizers.

Rick Brant agrees. "Reconciliation was what the games ended up being about, not just delivering an international sporting event."

Some Cowichan elders formed a drum group and offered their culture to people who really wanted to learn. The Cowichan Spirit Drummers is 100 drummers strong.

"I haven't seen that in any community across Canada. People are very typically concerned about giving away those traditional songs they hold so closely. But the elders understood it was an opportunity to share. It was really about creating friendships," says Rick.

Various community councils and organizations were inspired to continue building on the good works that the games had begun. Mark Buchanan and his team served on a few of those committees for a time, but some of the warmth generated by the games has turned chilly towards the New Life representatives. The dreaded term "hidden agenda" has been used.

"Actually, it's not that hidden," says Mark. "I think I may be a nuisance to some people. It's not hurting my feelings, but I don't have the time to negotiate it, because, indeed, ultimately our agendas may actually conflict. These committees are not the vehicles for what we are trying to accomplish. What we're pursuing these days is working collaboratively with Christians across denominations who share a vision for the kingdom of God in this community."

This collaboration has so far involved a furniture store, purchased by a group of Christian businesspeople who sell low-priced pieces and channel the profits towards programs that help First Nations at-risk youth. There are also opportunities for the teens to work at the store and receive practical training in sales and business.

Today, New Life continues with its many outreach programs, and responds to needs they see themselves, and as they are approached by the community. In the end though, it is still about relationships.

"We thought about what it would look like to have friends in the communities," says Mark. "We did a lot of teaching around that. It is servanthood, but not in this patronizing, condescending way. It is servanthood in the sense of finding out what are the genuine needs that we can come alongside. And we meet these needs while making friends and imparting dignity."

SOME OF WHAT THEY LEARNED ALONG THE WAY

- **When building bridges, don't go in evangelizing.** That will create obstacles from the get-go, says Mark. Concentrate on understanding the culture, the history and the current reality of your future friends.
- **Find out what is needed in your community.** Ask questions. Invite representatives from community groups to your church on a Sunday to speak and share what they do and what their needs are. Pray for them. Then thank them for coming and applaud them for their hard work in the community.
- **Leave partnerships gracefully, if that is what is required.** There may come a time when the agenda of community groups may veer away from the objectives of the Church. When New Life saw that, on

some committees at least, their presence was becoming an irritant and ultimately, there was a difference in agendas, they were fine with parting
ways in good cheer.

- **Determine how your church can mobilize for the
  long haul**, on a consistent basis and say, "This is
  our thing and we can do this." New Life did that
  and has simply built on it, time and time again.

MISSIONAL DISCUSSION

1. What are the issues in your community that bother
   you in that "remote, distant 'I wish somebody
   would do something about that kind-of-way'" that
   Mark Buchanan describes?
2. What values lie at the heart of the New Life approach to the restoration work they undertook?
   How might you apply these values in your setting?
3. New Life's experience working with community
   councils and organizations was mixed. What is
   your reaction to the accusation of Christians having
   "hidden agendas" in community work?

CHAPTER TWO
Neighbours

Coquitlam Alliance Church

_____

Coquitlam, B.C.
www.cachurch.ca

AVERAGE WEEKLY ATTENDANCE: 1,200
DENOMINATIONAL AFFILIATION: Christian and
    Missionary Alliance
YEAR FOUNDED: 1975

Most churches have a pretty good self-perception. In my travels across Canada as World Vision Canada's Director of Church Relations, almost everybody describes their congregation as being "friendly and warm," and as having a real "family feeling." This is probably true for most of the people in the congregation. Relationships are warm and have been in place for a long time. The worship service is a celebration of faith and of relationships.

It is reasonable to assume that those outside the church view the congregation in the same way. But I wonder how many congregations have no idea how they are actually perceived by their neighbours? Sometimes becoming missional might mean making amends, as well as making friends with those surrounding the church. This can be particularly important as a church ventures into new and challenging territory.

A positive self-perception is not always a reliable evaluation of a new initiative. What we think is a welcomed bridge into the community may in fact create a wall of resentment. Missional leaders are open to hearing the good, the bad and the ugly, so that the experience of God by their neighbours will be as unencumbered as possible.

Becoming missional may not be easy. A missional church focus will almost always lead us into unexpected, messy, but grace-filled places. God longs to restore relationships and repair justice. So where poverty and resource coexist, God will actively seek to bring them together; to build bridges between affluence and need. Both will benefit from the healing that comes when they are united together. The affluent requires opportunity to respond to need, to avoid the disease of self-centredness. While this is not often an easy process, there is no greater fulfillment for affluence than providing positive influence to a situation of need.

Getting in touch with what God is doing often requires honest assessment and a willing embrace of messiness.

—W.M.

▲   ▲   ▲

I expected it to be easy."

Even though that sounds suspiciously like famous last words, it is the first thing Rob Thiessen, a homelessness activist and member of Coquitlam Alliance Church in Coquitlam, B.C., says when asked about his experience establishing a Cold Wet Weather Mat program in his area.

Locals call the months between the first of November and the last of March the cold, wet weather season. The overcast skies and cold drizzle can be depressing for some people, but potentially awful for the homeless in the tri-city area of Coquitlam, Port Coquitlam and Port Moody, B.C. Rob was approached by a homelessness committee who knew he was "a church guy" and asked to draw in local churches to each provide one month's worth of free shelter and evening meals for the homeless in the tri-cities.

Rob's home church "jumped all over it." So did the other four churches he approached with the proposal. In fact, when Rob presented the idea to the other churches—of various sizes and denominations—he sensed a deep desire to serve their communities, but a bewilderment about how best to do it.

"Some of our churches were preaching all the right things, but had no impact on their local communities, and didn't know how they could," says Rob. "And they were afraid of homeless people. Some of the churches were embarrassed they hadn't thought of this on their own. We were fast asleep." It's only been in the last few years, says Rob, that area churches have realized that there are great needs "right under our noses. We were in a holy huddle, dead in the water, not making a bit of an influence in our community."

Churches recognized the program as a ready-made way to step into greater service to their own communities, something they were yearning to do—except for one detail. Their churches had to be rezoned, which involved public hearings and angry people who feared their neighbourhoods would "lose property value, have dirty needles all over the place, increased teenage pregnancy, disease and pandemics roaring through the neighbourhood," explains Rob. "There was very paranoid, phobic stuff that came out to the fore and was picked up by the media, and the debate became very public."

No neighbourhood was more organized, more vocal or more annoyed than the one surrounding Coquitlam Alliance, an active, growing congregation of 1,000 or so members who had no idea of the extent to which they had been irritating some of their neighbours over the years.

"It was a real eye-opener to us as a church," says Rob. "Some of the anger came from things we had done 15 years ago, like taking down trees to make a new parking lot, or blocking driveways during services."

One public council meeting to debate the rezoning started at 7 p.m. and finally, mercifully, ended at 3:30 in the morning. "The process became quite brutal with a very organized and loud resistance," says Rob.

The churches pushed back. The intensity of the heat forced the church leadership to defend their rationale for hosting such a program, including explaining their mission publicly and repeatedly to the city council, organized protesters and various nervous Nellies calling from around the neighbourhood.

"The church had to get up and start talking about what we did," says Rob "People had the impression that we were just a holy huddle, dressed up, singing, hearing someone preach and then going back home again every Sunday. People began finding out that we had been doing missional things forever, outside of our border, since the church started. We had to talk about the stuff we did and neighbours began to understand why our church would do this program."

David Wood is the senior associate pastor at Coquitlam Alliance. He welcomed the opportunity to interact with the community and help inform them about all that was going on at the church, including ministries such as Babyanne's Mansion Orphanage, a home and shelter for abandoned babies in the Philippines which was established by Coquitlam Alliance Church. The church also supports a pastor and Tarahumaran congregation in an isolated corner of a mountainous part of Mexico.

"The pastor tells us what he needs and we do it. We're not parachuting in and saying, 'We're going to build houses for a couple of families,'" explains David. "We're connected with someone local. They are leading the way and we are supporting them in whatever way we can."

The church has also done construction projects in Zambia and Indonesia, based on relationships they have nurtured with Christians in those countries, and a Food for the Homeless ministry makes and distributes 700 sandwiches to the homeless in the eastside.

Still, taking sandwiches to the eastside was different from bringing the homeless inside. But, after months of wrangling and debating, the nature of the phone calls began to change from outrage to cautious support. The rezoning was approved and the Cold Wet Weather Mat program began. Even those opposed to hosting the homeless in their own church building eventually came around.

"It made a mass change in the community. It really did raise up in our churches the question of what our responsibilities are in terms of social justice," says Rob. "It lit a fire that I don't think will go out any time soon. We need to take some chances and take some risks. We need to be in the middle of it."

Now, David Wood chuckles at the intensity of the initial backlash to the homeless program. "In the second year of the program, there was not a peep of protest. People who had been protesting it have joined in to help. That's a very cool story," says David.

Coquitlam Alliance has evolved from being a formidable missions force overseas—with a missions budget that has increased five-fold in recent years—to laying out mats on their church's floors to house the homeless in their own backyards.

"It's not like there's been a moment where we said 'Hey! We should care about the poor!" says David. "Every year we would pray as a staff about what we need to emphasize that year. We concluded that we really needed to have a heart for the poor and homeless, and do missions a little bit differently."

Coquitlam Alliance has moved from arms-length to hands-on. Which is what Rob Thiessen believes people really want anyway.

"Most people will step up and do stuff if you present them with a vision. We need that experience of hands-on. We've had so many people say that it's wonderful to serve the restaurant-style dinner presented to the men and women who sleep over at Coquitlam Alliance," says Rob. "Their previous experience had been writing a cheque every month. Some of us thought the homeless needed us, but it turns out that the churches needed the homeless."

According to David Wood, missional means that "the Church is doing what it was supposed to be doing all along, but we have a new word for it."

The word "missional" is a new one for Rob, not even appearing on his computer's dictionary—yet. But if it means that his own congregation has woken up to the needs they see around them and are responding, then it is all right with him.

SOME OF WHAT THEY LEARNED ALONG THE WAY

- **Keep your purpose in mind.** You may need to remind "fairly established Christian people what they are here for," says Rob. When Rob first introduced the idea of the Cold Wet Weather program in the tri-city churches he "used Jesus mostly, his parables and stories and life to show the risks he took. Jesus deliberately rubbed up against people others thought he should stay away from."

- **Build bridges, don't burn them.** You may not be a good neighbour and not even know it. Coquitlam Alliance was surprised to discover that they were sometimes burning bridges in their neighbourhood instead of building them. Issues like Sunday morning traffic and contentious landscaping decisions had alienated some of the people living around their building. The church grew in sensitivity to the daily lives of those around them, who may never choose to attend.

- **Communicate well.** The congregation realized that they had not been telling their story well. People who lived the closest to them did not understand what they were all about. "We had become irrelevant," says Rob. He advises a measured, cautious approach. "The Church needs to step up but not be shrill. But be loud enough. Internal communication was also crucial as the heat rose in the debate. "Let the church know how this is going to impact the community. It will change how people look at you," says Rob.

- **Nurture and support ministry ideas that originate with parishioners.** David Wood believes that "is a healthy thing that gives ownership."

MISSIONAL DISCUSSION

1. How do you suppose your church is perceived by the surrounding neighbourhood? What do you base your assumptions on?

2. Rob Thiessen mentions a fear of homeless people that existed within the congregations. What fears or hesitations to move outside the comfort zone can be found in your congregation?

3. What kinds of missional risks could your congregation take?

CHAPTER THREE
Entrepreneurs

People's Church

Grande Praire, Alta.
www.peopleschurch.cc

AVERAGE WEEKLY ATTENDANCE: 1,500
DENOMINATIONAL AFFILIATION: None
YEAR FOUNDED: 1981

Missional leadership is not for those wanting to make a name for themselves. It is about connecting people with the work of God. It is being able to admit that, as leaders, we do not always see everything that God is doing.

Every leader has blinds spots. These can be created by personal preference or individual style. Without a healthy self-awareness, leaders can slip into ruts and routines. But a healthy God-awareness helps leaders acknowledge that the activity of God is much broader than their personal preference or style. The task of the missional leader is not to get everyone on board with their vision, but rather to lead the way in understanding what God is doing and create the bold environment where people can get on board.

Leaders may be tempted to surround themselves with voices similar to their own. That way, support and encouragement to keep things going as they are is almost guaranteed. While this might make life easier, it does not create the environment where leaders can see beyond themselves and discover some undetected activity of God.

This is not to suggest that leaders surround themselves with negative people or empower the all-too frequent naysayers. However, empowering people to look in a different direction can open doors to discover an exciting new alignment with God's activity.

—W.M.

▲   ▲   ▲

A river runs through it—literally. The land where People's Church in Grande Prairie, Alta. is building a camp measures a mile by a mile by a mile, and is tucked just over the British Columbia border from this northern Alberta city, the fastest growing city in Canada.

The camp is named Kiskatinaw for the river that cuts it in half, and is one of the latest—and maybe one of the greatest—projects that People's Church has ever undertaken. The church's vision is to establish a place of retreat where families, church members and community members can relax, have fun and move deeper into their relationship with God and each other. Eventually, it will be staffed year-round and offer a lodge and cozy accommodations for people who want to get away by themselves, or ministry groups who believe in the power of the shared camp experience. Cross-country skiing, horseback riding and other activities will round it out.

"It is a beautiful setting," says Nelson Jones, head pastor of People's Church. "What we have there is something that will be for the Christian and for making their relational lives richer, but also very strongly for mission and bridge-building."

Nelson envisions the camp as a place of "intense ministry" that taps into the openness of just about everybody to have outdoor diversion. "People are open to camping, it's huge here. This provides us a natural place of achieving mission."

Achieving mission is what this church is all about. Nelson and his team recently invited a group of consultants to spend time at their church, an external evaluation process that he believes can help every congregation.

"You minimize those blind spots," says Nelson. "There's a point in your journey as a Christian leader where you understand that the call to serve Christ is a call to change who you are, to bring out of you all the stuff that He wants to, to heal all the stuff He must, and to make you a person who is constantly aware that your personal journey must lead you to greater effectiveness. That also means paying the cost in ego to reach the greater end."

In other words, leaders who are willing to make themselves vulnerable enough to have outside evaluations done

of their church and their leadership might not always hear
what they want to hear, but they will probably eventually
hear what they *need* to hear.

People's Church consultants met with church members, carefully chosen to reflect a variety of opinions, and
came back to the leadership team with an encouraging report.

"The consultant told us that usually mission statements
are on paper and then you find out something totally different," says Nelson. "But they told us that what we have
on paper is exactly what we are generating." The consultants also gave them the happy news that People's Church
per capita giving is one of the highest they have seen in
Canada. Good news, and rare news, for any church. "If your
mission statement is being realized, at least to a degree,
funds won't be your first issue to deal with. It creates an
energy and passion to give. I think there's a connection between those two things," says Nelson.

And at the same time that excitement builds over Kiskatinaw, another substantial missional project is getting
underway.The church is embarking on an ambitious building project that will be called The Family Reach Centre. It
is 19,000 square feet of fun that will include a full-sized
gymnasium, an activity area, and a cafe built in a loft that
will overlook both. It will be a multi-use site, but the main
thrust is providing new sports leagues to a city that is already fiercely athletic, especially in those long, winter
months.

"We're a northern city and this kind of facility makes a
heck of a lot of sense," says Nelson. There are already

sports facilities and leagues in Grande Prairie, but People's Church feel there is a space for something that is less expensive for families, and therefore accessible to a wider range of people. And the team behind the Family Reach Centre is very clear about who those people are. If you show up with your young athlete in tow to fill out the application and indicate that you attend another church in town, you go automatically onto the waiting list.

"If you're going to have a mission, you're going to have to deal with who is *not* your market," says Nelson. "If you don't do that in an intentional way, you will gravitate towards it. It's a matter of being just as intentional about who your market is not, as to who it is."

The market for the sports league is not church kids, even their own church kids, although they will be allowed to sign up—for now.

"We are giving our kids and families a chance to bring their non-Christian friends into this environment. The message will be to bring a friend. If they don't bring a friend, we may have to move to a policy on that," says Nelson. "It's a reverse of what you usually find in the church world. Usually, it's the Christian kids who show up."

The centre will be staffed with volunteers from the church and the teaching moments, as they arise, will be centred on character development in the participants. "This becomes a no-brainer for us. It's not about bringing them to an altar call. The idea is that these kids need character development, and yes of course, them coming to Christ. But that process will happen as you focus on the other, and it does work that way for us." says Nelson.

The other thing that works well for People's Church has been partnerships with groups like World Vision Canada. People's Church is a poster-child in World Vision's Globalink program that connects Canadian congregations with communities overseas. Globalink positions itself as a way for churches to "make a significant and lasting difference in the lives of people afflicted by poverty, malnutrition and HIV and AIDS." Churches commit to a three-year partnership and pledge that church members will sponsor, en masse, children from that one particular community.

Dale Jones is Nelson's assistant (and his nephew) and he likes what Globalink has empowered People's Church to do. "I like that you are affecting a community. I think it's clearer, what you are actually doing. You're helping an area, and all the children are being helped. We sponsor over 100 kids in this one community in Mali," says Dale. "As Christians, we need to reach out and be there for people who are in need. It is about meeting needs with love and letting God do His work."

For People's Church, the credibility, size and strength that World Vision brought to the table made them a natural fit for partnership. "I view it as imperative to the health of the church that it be working with organizations bigger and more specialized than itself, and be willing to have that type of partnership. We must recognize that there are things we can't do well, but they can. That is good for the heart of the church," says Nelson.

People's Church is also confident about what they can do quite well all by themselves. After attending a Kampala-based conference on HIV and AIDS in Uganda, People's put together a plan to support a group of pastors in that African nation who are working to improve life for their churches and communities. Pastors identify specific individuals from their churches who would be eligible for a micro-credit loan offered by People's Church. If the entire network of pastors approves, the small loan is offered. Participants who receive loans and attend churches are encouraged to tithe from their earnings, improving the life of their local church. Repaid loans go back into the pool of available funds, and on it goes in the typical micro-credit model. "This is life-changing for these people, to provide this capital to expand their businesses," says Nelson.

Meanwhile, People's Church has also helped the network of carefully selected pastors set up their own business—a 15-passenger van that serves as a taxi in traffic-congested Kampala. The pastors hire a driver and conductor. The income from that enterprise helps improve their own lives, and also goes into a fund to eventually purchase another vehicle and expand their fleet. The pastors receive supplements of approximately US$300 every three months to top up their salaries, directly from People's Church. Those same pastors have a "hidden door" on the website of People's Church where they can access the weekly teaching and receive learning and support.

The leadership team of People's Church bounce a lot of ideas around a long table in their church offices. "A lot of times," says Nelson, "the rest of them are further ahead on these things than I am. But we have a great passion to extend the church. That drives everything we do."

SOME OF WHAT THEY LEARNED ALONG THE WAY

- **Decide who your target group for ministry is** *not,* **and not just who it** *is.* People's Church is trying to resist the temptation to attract already churched kids into their upcoming sports programs by asking pointed questions on the registration form, and then creating a waiting list for kids who already attend churches in town.

- **"Is their DNA close to ours?"** That's the question People's Church asks of potential partners. "If it's not, they may still be a person or organization of character, but we don't want those types of relationships," says Nelson. "For example, if it's discipleship we would not want discipleship that services the saints, but rather, discipleship that matures the saints to service the Kingdom."

- **It's worth it to explore ready-made programs run by larger organizations** that your church can potentially tap into, as long as the DNA is similar.

- **When embarking on any partnership, consider these questions:**
  1. Who is this person/organization?
  2. Can they be trusted?
  3. What is the vision?
  4. What needs to be done?
  5. Can this person or group do it?

MISSIONAL DISCUSSION

1. How does your mission statement drive what you do?
2. Who is *not* your target group?
3. What could you do better with a partner? Better on your own?

CHAPTER FOUR
Risk-takers

Forest Grove Community Church

Saskatoon, Sask.
www.forestgrovecc.com

AVERAGE WEEKLY ATTENDANCE: 800
DENOMINATIONAL AFFILIATION: Mennonite Brethren
YEAR FOUNDED: 1964

Christianity has become a little too comfortable. We skim off the top when we give back to God. If we feel a little guilty, we may skim a little deeper.

But God continually invites us to empty ourselves, so that we can be filled up again. Once we experience the joy of being refilled, emptying ourselves becomes easier. But that first act of emptying is downright unnerving.

Going missional sounds exciting, but it can be disconcerting. When we get close to God's heart, we understand and feel God's extravagant love. God gives the best every single time. Grace in all its fullness is routinely made available and offered. When we seek to align ourselves with God's activity, we become aligned with the intention of God's heart. And that involves freely and extravagantly offering grace to areas of need.

The intention of God is to offer the best. To be the expression of God in any given situation, we must also be compelled to give the very best.

—W.M.

⋏   ⋏   ⋏

For many of us, when we donate used clothing to a ministry, it is the jeans with the tattered bottoms and the shirt with the tea stain that just won't come off. Linda Chamagne is the founder and director of The Bridge on 20th Street, an inner-city street ministry in Saskatoon. Linda is grateful for anybody who gives to The Bridge, but she says that at least half of the items should have gone straight to the garbage without passing Go.

Then one day, Bruce Enns, lead pastor of Forest Grove Community Church, a large Saskatoon congregation exploring what it means to be missional, showed up at The Bridge with his family and large cardboard boxes filled with his congregation's Sunday best. Inspired by an article in *Leadership* magazine, Bruce had wondered if it was "a nudging of God or our own foolishness" to ask his middle-class and up congregation to donate the money in their wallets, their coats and boots, and deposit them all at the front of the church during worship one Sunday. Their Sunday's best would be donated to The Bridge.

"The challenge was to give our best as worship to God," explains Bruce. "The response was overwhelming. Only two people knew I was going to do it, my wife and the worship pastor. I didn't want anyone else to know in case I bailed on the idea. But there was just a sea of people who came forward."

One man who didn't have any cash in his wallet left the service, drove to an ATM and came back with an envelope stuffed full. Another woman, who had finally bought the leather boots she had been eyeing for a shopping season or two, walked to the front of the church wearing those great boots and left only her coat as an offering. God called her on it as soon as she sat back down. The boots went too.

What Linda noticed first were the boxes that held the treasures. They were new boxes. That touched her deeply.

"I put a note on those boxes and told staff and volunteers not to touch them until I knew from the Lord what to do with them. I knew it was people's best, because in that setting, you wear your best to church. I felt there was a holiness around those boxes, a reverence. I didn't want to just open them up and let people rummage through them."

Linda and her crew set up a special room to showcase the donations. They filled clothing racks, with the items neatly organized into sizes. They laid out the shoes and the boots. When they were done, the room looked like a holy kind-of boutique. Then, in The Bridge's own Sunday service, they shared what Forest Grove had done and invited their visitors to enter the room in small groups where The Bridge's staff and volunteers helped them to carefully select items.

The dignity of it all was important to Linda. She is a woman who has been on the receiving end of help offered with dignity absent, strings strongly attached. Her husband was once turned away from a food bank because he didn't bring his own bag. It was their first visit and he didn't know he needed to.

That Sunday, says Linda, "our visitors were overwhelmed. They said things like 'I've always wanted a leather coat.' And 'I can't believe these boots fit me perfectly.' It was overwhelming." Linda was in tears for days.

"That was a powerful movement of God, I have no doubt about it," says Bruce. "But the challenge now is, 'how do we live out the missional life in a lifestyle?' That's what we've been wrestling with ever since."

Like any good wrestling match, sometimes you're pinned to the mat feeling a bit overwhelmed. Forest Grove has been dealing with the transition of moving from an attractional church to an intentionally missional model.

"Lots of great things have come out of the attractional model of 'if you build it, they will come,'" says Bruce, "and we want to be attractional and attractive, but it's so much more than that. How can we be a healthy, attractional church that becomes a base for missional movements?"

Missional writer Alan Hirsch's thinking helped Bruce shape his own. "Hirsch's whole premise is that the Church doesn't have a mission, but that God's mission has a Church. I really like that. God's Church is the vehicle for His mission. We don't want to just be a church that supports mission [and Forest Grove does that in abundance]—we want to be a church that is mission," says Bruce.

Church leadership has adapted how they chart church growth, moving from the old fashioned way of counting heads on Sunday mornings, to considering instead how many people are affiliated with Forest Grove through the weekly outreach activities of the church and its members. Its team of eight pastors decided to track all their ministry activities for one week, and what they found surprised them.

"What was interesting is that almost every person's involvement during a given week when we tracked it was with people who were unlikely to show up here on a Sunday morning," notes Bruce. "Missional means that can't matter quite as much. That can no longer be the be-all and end-all of what it means to be the Church."

So, one Sunday Forest Grove cancelled their services so parishioners could *be* the Church, instead of going to church. "It was to help our church understand more about what it means to be missional and that the church isn't only about Sunday morning gatherings. So, we cancelled a Sunday service just before Christmas, and told people that church wasn't cancelled, just the service was," explains Bruce. This idea was part of the Advent Conspiracy campaign that encourages Christians to spend less and give more during the Christmas season. Forest Grove folks were

encouraged to engage in simple acts of service or hospital-
ity, or whatever creative spin they came up with.

"Some went and helped in various settings, some went
and bought free coffee for everyone at a local restaurant,
some hosted brunches and invited neighbours," explains
Bruce.

Another time, the leadership cut a $500 cheque out of a
budget surplus for each of the 40 small groups at Forest
Grove. Groups were asked to be missional with it—to
move outside of their comfort zone of living rooms and "go
and be the church in Saskatoon." Some groups tried to give
it back. "They didn't want to *do* something," says Bruce.

But they did, eventually. "Giving them the money
forced them to wrestle with what God was calling them to
do. What's cool is that so many of the groups have stayed
connected with ministries in the city," says Bruce. "Missional helps with discipleship, because we've defined it as
Biblical learning, but it's actually about Biblical obedience.
It's not just knowing the word of God—it's living it out."

Forest Grove's shift to a missional emphasis has meant
that people who are more comfortable being spectators instead of participants might actually be getting a bit uncomfortable after all. Others, like busy mother Carol Metanc-
zuk, felt empowered to start their own ministry.

At a Forest Grove event, Carol really heard for the first
time that "... your life is your mission. Everyday can be your
mission field, you don't have to go anywhere. I thought that
was a great thing to think," says Carol. Together with her
friend Cathy, Carol decided to take one of the things they
were very good at—baking—and attended Saskatoon's

Farmer's Market every Saturday, selling focaccia bread and cube-cakes (square cupcakes) to raise money for charities.

Forest Grove did not just dump shiny new boxes full of Sunday's best off at The Bridge. That encounter, and many conversations later, have led to a partnership—on paper even—for how Forest Grove can enter into the life of The Bridge, and vice-versa. There will be financial support, but there will also be a coming alongside that feels like it is more missional than even the giving-the-dress-shirt-off-your-back moment that began this whole relationship.

"I believe it had a lasting impact," says Linda. "Forest Grove is a church that has put in a lot of hours developing a partnership with us. It is more than just writing a cheque, or volunteers dropping in. It is a tangible agreement."

For Linda, what makes Forest Grove stand out is that they asked what would be most beneficial for The Bridge. And then they listened to the answer.

"People will say to you, 'What do you need?' and then they give what they want," says Linda. "I'm not knocking the Church, I love the Church. But it's like when you ask someone how they are but you don't really mean it or don't really want to know. Forest Grove putting this on paper and having an agreement with us is a big thing for us. This is more than financial support. This is 'How can we bless you? How can we be blessed?' A partnership is a two-way street."

The emphasis on building long-term partnerships is part of Forest Grove's global vision as well. The church has been sending mission teams to Panama for years, and will continue to build on the work they have accomplished there.

"Being missional isn't a shotgun approach to a whole bunch of random things. What's more impactful are the ongoing partnerships," says Bruce.

SOME OF WHAT THEY LEARNED ALONG THE WAY

- **Communication is critical.** Bruce Enns notes that the latest church terms are often used differently and interchangeably, and that can be confusing. "Missional" gets mixed up with "emerging" for example. The Forest Grove ministry team has been deliberate in communicating from the pulpit and through mass emails, stories and newsletters so that the congregation knows exactly what lies behind the words that are used.

- **An emphasis on the "church dispersed"** throughout the week—instead of the Sunday morning worship service being viewed as where church really happens—has helped spread the message that every member is on a mission, 24/7.

- **Put it in writing.** When Forest Grove develops partnerships with other organizations or individuals, they capture it in writing, creating a covenant that reminds both parties of the how, the when and the why of what they are working for together.

- **Celebrate.** Tell missional stories often. People want to be a part of something that is faithful, world-changing and sometimes even fun.

MISSIONAL DISCUSSION

1. What bold and unexpected moves has your church made, or would consider making, in an effort to be missional?
2. What long-term partnerships could you enter into—locally, nationally and globally?
3. How could missional outreach help with discipleship of your church members?

CHAPTER FIVE
Encouragers

Winkler Mennonite Brethren Church

Winkler, Man.

www.inspireequipemerge.com

AVERAGE WEEKLY ATTENDANCE: 600
DENOMINATIONAL AFFILIATION: Mennonite Brethren
YEAR FOUNDED: 1888

A missional church leader recognizes that the activity of God does not revolve around leadership. God responds to open hearts, not to fame or recognition.

Perhaps the greatest measure of leadership is not accomplishment, but empowering others in a mutual attempt to bring focus to the activity of God. Perhaps the greatest gift of the missional church concept is the transformation of the ordinary into the extraordinary. It is the recognition that the remarkable, redemptive activity of God can be

found in the most mundane settings and regular activities. God revolu-
tionizes the ordinary.

Missional church leaders develop a new way of looking, seeing and
hearing. They develop a missional sense—a new way of perceiving the
activity of God around them. Missional church leaders begin to recog-
nize that God may be actively working through the parishioner you
would least expect or in an ordinary context you would not initially
think of. This readiness to see and align with God's activity could re-
sult in an unexpected and unanticipated ministry.

—W.M.

⚑   ⚑   ⚑

Winkler, Manitoba, is the place "where people make the difference." That's one of the mottos of this Prairie city, founded in the late 1800s by Mennonites on the run. With a population of 9,106, Winkler advertises itself as a place of hard work, friendly people and faith-based values. And if Canada does have a Bible belt, then Winkler is the "shiny part of the buckle," according to Terry Dueck, associate pastor of missions and community for Winkler Mennonite Brethren Church (WMBC).

WMBC is Canada's oldest Mennonite Brethren (MB) church, tracing its origins back to a baptism party in the Dead Horse Creek in 1886. That group grew to 16 members who organized themselves into the first MB Church in

Canada a few years later. Today, the church numbers around 600. Increasingly, there is both need and opportunity for WMBC to serve Winkler directly, as well as inner-city Winnipeg, long considered a mission field for this congregation.

"Our church has a good understanding of moving in the direction of coming alongside what God is doing, standing with the broken and the hurting. It's this idea of incarnational living," explains Terry.

Most churches are used to the idea of incarnating themselves thousands of miles away on a short-term mission trip or some other kind of international outreach. WMBC runs programs in Mexico and India, partnering with organizations like Christian Camps International. But WMBC has found a way to go missional locally—in the used car business of all things—a way of being missional that did not have a blueprint attached.

It started when Chad Berg, a WMBC member, was done with his stint teaching Sunday School. He had his fill leading youth group and completed his rotation of all the other normal stuff faithful Christians do to serve God and be involved in the life and work of their church.

"Not saying that teaching Sunday School wasn't good, but there are those things that grab hold of you and you say 'Yes! This is what I was created for!'" says Chad. Every church has people sitting in the pews who don't see how their personal gifts or skill sets could possibly be used within the context of the church service itself. Chad was one of them.

Chad, a licensed mechanic, had begun to notice that the problems of inner-city Winnipeg were inching closer to Winkler. As he wandered through his auto repair shop, he often wondered if God could actually use his gifts and skills as a car guy. There was increasing unemployment in town, more visible signs of addiction, and more and more people coming into Chad's Auto Repair Shop to get their cars fixed, and then not being able to pay the bills.

"It's not like they were doing it intentionally," says Chad. "But these people need help. Figuring out how to help was where my heart was." Chad kept dreaming, praying and talking to the leadership at WMBC.

Then, one day, as casually as some people drop off a bag of used clothes, someone dropped off a car at the church as a donation. A week or so later, someone in need asked for a car to use. That was the sign that Chad and his church were waiting for, to launch G-Force, a program that puts dependable cars into the hands of people and families in need. G-Force puts wheels on being missional. At last count, G-Force has had 150 cars donated to their fleet.

"When a person wants to donate a vehicle to the church, they bring it down, sign the papers over and have an appraiser assess the value," explains Chad. The donor receives a tax receipt at the end of the year for the value of the donation. Chad and a team of volunteers—including some of Chad's own employees who volunteer a night a week as well as individuals from other Winkler churches—go through the car and determine what repairs it needs.

Chad sells the parts to the church at cost and the car is fixed up by the volunteer staff. It is then inspected by the Manitoba Safety Inspection and deemed road-worthy before being put back in circulation.

"The next step is to get it to people in need. As people build relationships with others in the community, they find the people in need," says Chad. "And they steer them towards G-Force."

G-Force doesn't advertise, because they believe they would be flooded with requests. Besides, relationships are key to this ministry. "We deal with a lot of messy situations," explains associate pastor Terry. "We prefer to err on the side of grace. But part of it is walking alongside people and helping them learn to make better choices. It's never straightforward."

The church realizes that handing over a car to someone may not solve the deeper issues in their life. "We try and find out where they are," says Chad. "Are they working? Do they have kids? Do they have health concerns?"

A skilled mentor from the church volunteers to work with the individuals and families to sort through their budget and determine if they have funds available to put fuel in the car, to register it and if it's actually going to be a help instead of just another burden to carry.

"We want to know that they want to improve their current situation," explains Chad. "It's our way of understanding how to help them best."

In a small town like Winkler, without the transportation services available in a city, having access to a dependable vehicle means that people can make it to work on

time, transport their kids to healthy, extra-curricular activities, or make it to a job interview that might actually
change their lives.

"We sign an exclusive use agreement with them that
they can use the car that belongs to the church. It's almost
like we're a leasing company. They can't sell it and must
agree to maintain it. We walk alongside them, and if the
car needs more work in the future, we give them free la-
bour," explains Chad.

When the recipient of the car feels they are ready to
move on, they can purchase the vehicle or return it, and the
process begins again with that car now available for another family.

"We've had about five vehicles given back and the people have moved on to better circumstances," says Chad.
"We call those success stories."

For the leadership of WMBC, this entire ministry has
been a success story.

"One of our mission statements," says Terry, "is to pas-
sionately lead people to love and follow Jesus. This ministry keys in on the passion of one person following their
dreams, and giving and serving creatively. This one individual had the courage to step out and do something that
wasn't quite the norm and doesn't quite fit into what we
think of as 'normal' church ministries."

For Chad, the whole experience has been "a major
boost. I've come to see that you can't put God into a box.
There are ways of reaching people that mean we have to
think beyond your typical Sunday School classroom. We
have to change the idea that if we can only get them into

Sunday School, we're going to change their lives. It's not like that."

Chad says that people are surprised the church is willing to give them cars. What they expect is a blessing and a cheery wish that things will get better for them soon. "This has really struck me," says Chad. "We find out people are in need of a car, and instead of just saying 'Well, we hope you find one,' we are able to help out where they are."

Chad and WMBC discovered that having an outside of the box ministry also unleashed the energy of a group of people who didn't exactly fit into the box themselves. "When I think of the people involved in the repair end of things, they have struggled to find their place in the church," says Chad. "They don't have the characteristics or the desire to teach. They can't sing in the choir because they can't sing. They don't like to be around a lot of people, so working with the youth doesn't work. But, you know what, they really like to fix cars. They finally feel plugged in."

It encourages people, says Chad, to know that the Christian life is not just dressing nicely on Sunday morning, "but it's Thursday night too, when you're fixing cars."

G-Force has welcomed the help of members from other churches who love the idea. "We want it to be a community effort, and not just a WMBC thing," says Chad.

So, if someone has an idea that sounds a little bit crazy, it just might be God's to begin with.

"Pray, pray, pray," advises Chad. "And talk to others about it. Share your dream. It may be that someone else is dreaming a similar dream. I thought at first it was just a really crazy idea, but when others heard about it, there was a little sparkle in their eye that said, 'Yeah, that would be cool.'"

Recently, another member of WMBC dropped into Terry's office. "He's a contractor, a builder who says he's seen what Chad has done with his gifts, and he's wondering what he could do with his own," says Terry. "Our role is not to hold people back when they say 'Here are my gifts, here are my interests.' It's to free them. Give people the freedom to say 'We are the Church.'"

SOME OF WHAT THEY LEARNED ALONG THE WAY

- **Find common ground.** The most effective missional ministries seem to be built on that common ground where the needs of the larger community and the gifts and skills of the church community meet. Church members who are not currently engaged in a ministry may not yet see the connection between their gifts and opportunities to serve.
- **Empowering leadership** is key to releasing the gifts of a congregation. Terry Dueck's ministry style includes an open door where church members feel welcome to come in and pitch an idea, knowing they will receive honest feedback, encouragement and support. The church leadership at WMBC did not take over G-Force, but they supported and nurtured it.

- **Use successful ministry models and then tweak them.** Chad was aware of a Willow Creek auto ministry. It inspired him, but it still wasn't quite what he had in mind. Ministry entrepreneurs take the best of what has been done before them, but then tweak it to fit their own gifts, available resources and community needs.

- **Seek God's guidance and confirmation.** Encourage people to pray and ask God to show them their gifts and how they can be used in a completely new way. The holy imagination can dream up schemes that can change the world. It always has.

MISSIONAL DISCUSSION

1. Who in your church congregation doesn't necessarily fit into traditional church ministry, but might be open and ready for missional living?

2. What is the potential for "outside of the box" ministries in your congregation and in your community?

3. How could your leadership be leveraged to encourage ministry ideas that come from church members?

CHAPTER SIX
Welcomers

The Table

Winnipeg, Man.

AVERAGE WEEKLY ATTENDANCE: 65

DENOMINATIONAL AFFILIATION: Evangelical Covenant
    Church of Canada

YEAR FOUNDED: 2000

Going missional is about kingdom growth. This sounds easy enough, but it is, in fact, quite difficult and disconcerting for most congregations, because God is busy building the kingdom in unconventional ways.

A new church that is just starting out may have to grapple with who it is that extends the invitation for others to join. Often, the church is seen as the inviting body, offering people an opportunity to discover God and experience God's grace. But the missional approach acknowledges that it is God—not the Church—who extends the invitation.

This is an important distinction. If the Church sees itself as the host of the party, then it feels compelled to shape the guest list. Criteria are developed. Guidelines are written. But if we understand God to be the One responsible for issuing the invitation, then the Church is removed from the responsibility of guarding the guest list. The invitation is for everyone to receive God's mercy and experience God's transforming embrace.

The task of the Church in this missional understanding is to welcome whomever God has invited—and to eat joyfully with those we find at the table.

—W.M.

▲   ▲   ▲

On any other day of the week, the round bar table in the middle of The Academy Bar and Eatery in Osborne Village in Winnipeg might hold an order of Rajun Cajun Quesadillas, Artichoke Mascarpone Bruscetta or maybe just that good old pub fare, nachos and beer.

But on Sundays, things are different. There's a loaf of bread in the middle of the table, broken in two. Two chalices filled with Welch's grape juice are set out for whoever would like to eat and drink at The Table, a church that meets on Sunday mornings in this bar in Winnipeg's most densely populated neighbourhood.

Osborne Village is populated indeed, with enough tat-too parlours to give any mother a nightmare, funky shops, art galleries and people that are so cool one could become quickly aware of one's own un-coolness.

It's that section of town that most big cities have, genu-inely shabby chic for years, but slowly being sat up straight and polished by young professionals and retirees who see its charm and want a bit of it as their own. Winnipeg's *Up-town Magazine* named Osborne Village as the best place to live in 2008.

That's just about the time that Gerald Froese, a 56-year-old Winnipeg pastor with years of traditional church services under his belt, named it the best place to start a church in a bar with a group of like-minded believers.

"It's been our picture and our hope that we would grow a community in the heart of the city," explains Gerald. "Osborne has been an alternative community for years now. Squeegee kids are here, now young professionals and a host of retired folks. The condos have gone up here now and only they can afford them."

Gerald is as surprised as anybody that he and his team are leading a church in a bar. He remembers working with a youth pastor years ago, who had spent time in England and returned to Canada all fired up about churches meet-ing in pubs.

"At the time, I remember thinking 'Thank God I will be long gone before they are doing that here. This was not part of my plan or design.'"

But he's pretty sure that he has happened upon one of those quiet things that God had in mind. "We want to grow a community that loves God, that loves the Osborne community. We're trying to call people to the Lord's table, to God, and to our table. We want to build community here. We're trying to set the table in Osborne in such a way that they will want to come."

The vibe of the service is casual, low-key and welcoming. Kids are few at the moment, so they stay in the service. "One set of parents said that we need to think about spiritual formation for children, but they don't want their kid locked up in a basement, like they were," says Gerald.

The teaching is conversational and the style of worship music changes from week to week, depending on who is playing and leading. Music, in fact, sits at the head of this table. "Music is a big part of our church. We did a Beatle's Night on a Thursday and 340 people showed up." The evening was sponsored by The Table and broke records at The Academy for food and drink sales.

If people have heard about the church in the community, it's usually because of the music. Styles vary week by week, some of the worship leaders are well known in the Christian community, others not so much. Some just play a mean riff on a guitar

"In my conversations with our guests, there is often some kind of interest point or someone they know—or, they've heard about the music. Because this is an artistic community, music is a big deal," says Gerald. "I've met several people who are professional musicians who don't do church, but they may know the artist who is leading on a Sunday, and so they come because they know the guys up-front. Music is the thing we can do, and that's the train I'm riding."

The bar table that is used for communion on Sunday mornings even sits in the middle of the dance floor. "We wanted it to be central," explains Gerald. "We say 'Come, this is the place to receive grace. This is the place to receive hope.'" Gerald refers to the table during his talks, but has dispensed with the more traditional blessing of the elements prior to communion. "I tell people that the table is set for us to meet with God."

People can wander up, eat from the bread and drink from the chalice at any point during the service—when the Spirit leads them, literally. The Table is a witness that "God is close. He is here. He is as close as this table and you can come to this table and meet with Him," explains Gerald.

The vision for the table as a central symbol for the church comes from Luke 10. Jesus has already moved the 12 disciples out the door, then he gets down to the business of sending out 72 more, two by two. Jesus gives them their walking orders: When you enter a town and are welcomed, eat what is set before you. Heal the sick who are there and tell them, 'The kingdom of God is near you.'

That's what Gerald says The Table is trying to accomplish in Osborne Village. Eating what is before them and then setting their own table and inviting anyone to join them.

"Anyone" is an important word. Set up church in a bar and you just might be rubbing elbows with people that you wouldn't otherwise hang out with. Theological and lifestyle challenges are probably on the horizon. Gerald is a firm believer that being part of a community that is teaching the Bible in a non-threatening way is the best way to bring about healthy change in people's lives.

"We are in training on this. We're still trying to figure it out. But when you say you are missional then if we're not going to open the doors to people, to join in their lives to bring hope and health and healing, then we might as well just lock our doors," says Gerald.

Tim Plett agrees. He is a 48-year-old pastor who spoke a few times at The Table and decided he liked it enough to be on the staff. Tim resonated with what he calls the "fluidity" of ethos of The Table.

"We are a community still becoming. We are asking the missional questions first, instead of the self-serving questions. The community is about working hard to engage the Story actively in the present cultural context. We find that exciting. I find that essential," Tim explains.

For Tim, the question of clashing lifestyles and theologies that might arise when not just everyone—but absolutely anyone—is truly welcome *just as they are*, belongs in the category of margins, whether it is a same-sex couple or seniors who want to live together without being married so they don't lose their benefits. Tim says that is an issue that is less contentious than some, but still problematic pastorally.

Tim references Old Testament scholar Walter Bruggemann who writes that there should be no constraints on who the community welcomes, because there are no constraints on who the gospel welcomes. Tim acknowledges that, especially in the evangelical sub-culture of the Canadian Church, these are big questions which have to do with "our understanding of truth, our understanding of how we value community discernment and how authoritative we understand that discernment to be. For some people, I just pushed a big boulder down the hill and it won't stop till somebody dies. But we can't be missional if the comfort of our parishioners is our priority. The goal is not comfort—the goal is formation."

The variety of people who wander into The Table tells Gerald and Tim that there is a need out there for this kind of a church, in this kind of a neighbourhood, in any kind of a bar.

"I have nothing against traditional church," says Gerald. "I have no axe to grind. But sitting in the back pews of every church are people who are not engaged and have been there for years. They are people who may get excited about doing church in a slightly different way."

Often, when risk-taking Christ-followers start a new church doing things in new ways, it is easy to fall back onto the default measuring stick of pastoral success: numbers of behinds in the pews, or in The Table's case, bar stools. That doesn't do much for the guys in the bar.

"As a ministry professional, I am now at a place where, honestly, I'd rather have the right 50 people there," says Tim. "I did Big Church. I've been there, done that. And I left it pretty empty."

If The Table tops off at 150, Tim and Gerald would be happy. "That's about the amount of people you can know," says Tim. "Much more than that and you can't know and you aren't known. A little community like ours is working hard to say that being missional is an everyday part of life. And what form of gathering that comes out of that is up for grabs."

The word "missional" doesn't actually get used much around The Table. "'Organic' is more the word that we use in our leadership gatherings," says Gerald, "but missional is the journey we are on."

It's a journey that started with a question: "What is happening in this community already, and how can we be a part of it?" The answer they came up with, for now, is mixed up somewhere in music, in a bar, in even tougher questions that dance around margins and mercy, and on a table that—for the rest of the week anyway—looks just like any other table. But on Sunday, it offers up something different.

SOME OF WHAT THEY LEARNED ALONG THE WAY

- **Be open to change.** Even though the idea of open communion set up on a bar table seems to capture what The Table is all about, even that is not set in stone. The leadership of The Table are open to in-spiring ideas for approaching God and community that members or visitors may bring forward. They see themselves as a community evolving, and that's a positive for them.

- **Don't be afraid to dream the crazy dream.** "I've been dreaming about taking this show on the road," says Gerald Froese. "If this experiment works, maybe there are other cities where we can do a church in a bar."

- **Failure may be a part of the success.** The Table offered music nights on Sunday nights, and they were a flop. "We thought Sunday nights would be a home run," says Gerald. "They weren't. The owner said to shut it down. Turns out, Thursday nights did the trick." Be willing to experiment, then move on to your next best plan if the first one doesn't work.

- **Listen.** Get to know the community you are in. What are people interested in? Ask the question: What is God doing here?

- **Be prepared for resistance.** When you begin a unique expression of church, it won't be for everybody. There will be people who would say "This is chaos, get me out of here," says Tim.

MISSIONAL DISCUSSION

1. Tim Plett argues that "we can't be missional if the comfort of our parishioners is our priority. The goal is not comfort—the goal is formation." How strong are the "comfort expectations" in your church?

2. Leaders at The Table describe their ethos and worship style as fluid. What freedoms do you see, and what challenges?

3. How can your church become more welcoming and less guarded when "anyone" walks in the door?

CHAPTER SEVEN
Servants

Riverwood Community Church

Winnipeg, Man.
www.riverwood.cc

AVERAGE WEEKLY ATTENDANCE: 1,000

DENOMINATIONAL AFFILIATION: Independent

YEAR FOUNDED: 1995 (Easter Sunday)

The Church always wants to see people find new life, as it should. But the missional church will truly become aligned with God's invitational activity without demanding results. To be missional is to accept the same chance of success that God accepts. And with God, whether a positive response is generated or not, grace and mercy is always offered.

If we genuinely want to see as many people as possible experience new life in Christ, the church should always be looking for ways of better communicating God's love. But the missional church will not stop expressing love and serving others even if no one comes to faith. It will be unrelenting in freely expressing love, offering mercy and extending grace - with no strings attached, and no demands of response associated with the activity. But there will be a prayerful yearning for people to open themselves up more fully to the God who longs to restore and redeem.

The beautiful thing about being aligned with God's relentless offer of grace is that such communities do, in fact, attract. The best invitation for coming to church is when a member of the congregation is truly excited by their own congregation. Their love of their church shows as their face beams with excitement. Without even knowing it, that can be the most attractive invitation of them all.

When aligned with God's invitational activity, churches will be fervent in their practical expressions of love and mercy. The missional church is not only excited about aligning with God, but it will also be ready to embrace the possibility of what might appear to be fruitless activity. Whether it is received or not, missional churches offer the unmistakable expression of God's love. And as we know, God's love and grace are irresistible.

—W.M.

▲   ▲   ▲

The congregation at Riverwood Community Church in Winnipeg likes to catch people off-guard. Once granted the dubious distinction of being "the ugliest church in Winnipeg," the church has a super casual vibe—from the coffee that is available anytime to their tagline "faded jeans and broken people welcome." Faded jeans can be found anywhere, and broken people are clearly everywhere—but both happen to be in abundance in Elmwood, the corner of Winnipeg where Riverwood makes its home.

Elmwood is a neighbourhood of the working poor, with one of the highest teen pregnancy rates in Manitoba. Sometimes it's rough. It's always tough. Then there is this quirky, funky, edgy church on Riverton Avenue that insists anyone can come exactly as they are and that it has something to offer that is life-changing and practical to the point of painful: This is, after all, a church that will clean up your dog poop.

Yes, it's true. An essential element of what lead pastor Todd Petkau calls this "intensely missional" church is Adopt-A-Block. Todd and his team adapted the idea from Matthew Barnett's The Dream Centre, a large, making waves kind-of church in Los Angeles. The guiding principle is that cities are in a mess, and churches can impact the broken and hurting through acts of practical service.

The Dream Centre takes it to another level with a sponsor-a-block model, not unlike the sponsor-a-child model used by many charities. Riverwood instead focuses on church teams who are committed to visiting blocks of houses and offering to help the residents with whatever practical jobs they might have that need to be done.

"We have a team of 25 or so that go out to 150 homes every other Saturday," explains Todd. "Our philosophy is that we are not here to get you to believe anything or to read anything. We are simply asking them if we can serve them in some way."

People sometimes think they are nuts, at least at first. "People are reluctant to ask for help. Then we walk up to the house and say 'Hey, we're from Riverwood, the church down the road. You may have heard of us. Can we do anything to help you in any way?' They say no. Then, we might say 'Well, it looks like you have a couple of big dogs, can we clean up your dog poop?'"

Anyone who owns a dog knows that this kind of offer is unprecedented, a God-send, pretty much a miracle—and a tough one to turn down.

"They say, 'Go ahead, if you want to,'" says Todd, "and then wonder, 'Who are these insane people?'"

The team returns in two weeks, with a fresh offer to help—depending on the weather, they'll bring along a lawn mower, a shovel, a rake, whatever. As word spreads, they do get the overly optimistic person calling the church office wanting a new roof put on their house, but the church explains that they are just a group of people trying to share Christ's love in a practical way.

"The measure of success of Adopt-A-Block is if we managed to give the love of Christ away, not if we get them into our church," says Todd. "We're not trying to manipulate or trick people into church. If they never come to church, that is fine."

Todd says that having a team of volunteers who truly accepts that filling seats in the building is not the goal takes the pressure off. The volunteers relax and are more genuine and enthusiastic. It just feels better. It's not sneaky.

"Would we like every person we connect with to get connected with a local body and give their life to Christ?" asks Todd. "Of course, we would love that. The key is that when we feel we are giving a box of oranges away just to get someone in the door of the church, it becomes very shady and our motives are off."

Of course, hearts *do* change and so do lives. Being genuine often has that kind of impact, whether it's planned or not. Susan is one of those stories. Todd was on that particular Adopt-A-Block team and offered to chip the Winnipeg ice off her front steps. They did small jobs for Susan for a year.

"A couple of weeks in, she asked if we had a choir. I told her that we weren't a choir kind of church, but that we did happen to have one choir specially formed for Christmas." Susan asked if she could join it. She was warmly welcomed into the choir, where, according to Todd, "everyone just loved on her." Six months later, she came to Christ and Todd had the privilege of baptizing her.

"It's about being patient," says Todd. "We think of these acts of service as a moment when people are being caught off-guard and their hearts are being opened. We believe the Holy Spirit comes along and deposits a seed. Some of them take root, others don't. But our job is to plant those seeds."

Which they literally did during a one-day outreach blitz called Love Winnipeg. Riverwood showed up on one worn-down street with a dump truck full of top soil and two flatbeds full of flowers. They went door to door asking for help getting rid of the soil and the flowers. Neighbours obliged and an entire block was made beautiful in one afternoon. The Riverwood team ended the day with a barbeque for the street.

"It had the feeling of an extreme home makeover," says Todd. "We wore matching T-shirts, and neighbours were meeting neighbours."

Trash Talk Sunday was another missional blitz. Riverwood volunteers went door-to-door offering to gather up and take away trash, or large items destined for the dump that normal city removal services wouldn't take. Everything was transported to the parking lot at Riverwood and served as a huge object lesson for the community: This is a church that wants your junk. You can come just as you are (remember, faded jeans, broken people). Your life doesn't have to be cleaned up first. Then, Riverwood hired three unemployed Elmwood men to finish the job and make a run to the dump.

Riverwood expects that if 1,000 people are sitting in Sunday morning seats, then 1,000 pairs of hands will eventually be engaged in hands-on missional service to the community. The leadership team routinely presents "first-serve opportunities" to the church body.

"You're here, so do something," is a message that is repeated often. A few times a year, Todd and his team will preach a rousing call to service. "I will say that if people are coming to this place because there is good music and good drama, then they are taking up a seat that someone else could use," says Todd. "We're not into the show. We're here to help people find their place of serving."

That's exactly what Rick Lange, a Winnipeg cop for more than 27 years, was waiting to hear. When he listened to Todd say that if you weren't here to engage, then you were probably in the wrong place, he knew he was in just the right place.

"That was exactly what I wanted. A 24/7 type of Christianity. It is fun to just sit there, I'm not saying that it's not fun. When we have that kind of mind-set we separate our Christian life from the rest of our life. We separate what we are," says Rick. "But with a missional church, I am living this all the time. I'm here for God's use all the time."

The opportunities for serving through Riverwood are plentiful. The church runs Hope Store, offering used toasters and frying pans, shirts and skirts, skates and sleds to the working-poor neighbourhood. The Refuge is a drop-in group for young mothers, mostly teens who wouldn't venture in on a Sunday morning. "It's their connecting place," says Todd. Their evening includes a God-talk, life-training sessions and then time with their very own mentor, a Riverwood volunteer.

Recovery ministries like Divorce Care and 12-step programs are growing. Riverwood realized they presented themselves as a place for broken people, but didn't offer a lot of practical ways to get whole again. "We had this mantra of faded jeans and broken people, and we felt convicted that this phrase had inspired a lot of people. But once they got here, we didn't know what to do with them. Our mantra didn't have teeth," says Todd. Now, it's starting to.

Vivian Wall is a Riverwood volunteer who works with a Tuesday night drop-in for kids in the neighbourhood, many of them from the Adopt-A-Block program. Vivian quit church for 15 years before she found Riverwood, and discovered a way of being Christian that made more sense to her than what she had experienced in her childhood. "I grew up in a church family, very evangelical. But for those in that generation, church was about being inside those four walls. It's very different now. You see how people are transformed when they realize that this is what the gospel is. It's not about us and them. It's about who we are created to be."

This kind of intentional relationship-building is foundational, but not perfect. We are, after all, on this side of kingdom come.

"Unfortunately, there is still the 'we' and 'them'—us in the church and them in the community. We really try and fight that though," says Vivian. "It is our community, and that means *all* of us. There is a constant line you have to bring down. That's an interesting challenge we have. There's also the whole spiritual pride thing. The ground is level at the foot of the cross," says Vivian. "Regardless of the teaching you get, you're going to have people bring their own stuff into it. So, you pray, and ask God to transform hearts." And then, at least at Riverwood, you get moving.

Todd calls Riverwood "Elmwood-centric" in its focus. The church will never leave the neighbourhood for the suburbs. In fact, a lot of suburbanites—including Vivian—drive a fair distance to attend Riverwood. They are attracted to the community of giving within a community of need, and they want to be a part of it.

A milestone moment for many Canadian churches on the missional journey is the recognition that our own surrounding communities are mission fields of opportunity for practical service in Jesus' name—that mission does not just mean going overseas. A mission trip can mean every moment you spend out of your bed.

For churches like Riverwood who see themselves as "strategically called to a disadvantaged community, the need was obvious," says Todd. "When you are in the suburb and you think of mission, you tend to think of global. It's less obvious."

However, that does not mean Riverwood is not global in its reach as well. Tom Davis' book *Red Letters*, a call to the Church to live out Jesus' words to care for the poor, especially those with HIV and AIDS, lit a fire under Todd. He called Davis and asked for his help connecting Riverwood with a community in need in Africa. A relationship with a community in Swaziland is growing, including members of Riverwood sponsoring close to 140 children. The church also supports an orphanage in Mexico and has made work trips that include some of the young moms who attend the Refuge drop-in hosted by Riverwood.

"We're just trying to figure this whole missional thing out," says Todd. "I know how poor we are at this thing, but we're trying. That's the key."

People and churches who are as intensely missional as Riverwood tire pretty quickly of talking about how missional they are. It can be seen as the latest word, the newest Church thing, when, of course, it's one of the oldest Church things.

"This whole conversation about being attractional or being missional. We might be really naive here, but why can't we be both? Wouldn't it be great to be attractional, in that people know that they are safe and loved here, that there is something that is attracting me here?" asks Todd. Great question.

SOME OF WHAT THEY LEARNED ALONG THE WAY

- **Connecting with others** on the missional journey has been important for Riverwood. The Dream House in Los Angeles and the book *Red Letters*, among others, provided the Riverwood leadership with models they could adapt for their own community. They didn't hesitate to call the author of *Red Letters* and ask for his help directly. He was happy to oblige.
- **Don't be afraid to preach a message that is hard to hear.** When Todd and his team preach that if you're not going to serve, you're taking up a seat that someone else could use, it can be uncomfortable. But for some people, it's what they've been waiting to hear their whole Christian lives. The team also points out that if you are in need of healing and rest, that's okay too. You are in a safe place.
- **Provide practical information.** The Riverwood website presents opportunities to serve that read

like actual job descriptions, listing time commit-
ments and requirements. People know what opportunities are available without even having to ask.

MISSIONAL DISCUSSION

1. To what extent do the people in your church reflect
   the people in your community and vice versa?
2. "If they never come to church, that's fine." says
   Todd Petkau. How would your church respond to
   an outreach activity that was not primarily about
   getting people to church?
3. How could you build a bridge between the "we"
   and the "them" mentioned by Vivian?

CHAPTER EIGHT
Connectors

Christ Church
_____
Oshawa, Ont.
www.christchurchoshawa.org

AVERAGE WEEKLY ATTENDANCE: 175
DENOMINATIONAL AFFILIATION: Anglican Church of
   Canada
YEAR FOUNDED: 1928

Being aligned with God is being sensitive and attuned to the needs of others. Where you find need, you will also discover the desire and intent of God to respond. To understand what is happening in your community is to discover the need of the community—and therefore, the activity of God.

Churches can fall into a trap of thinking that they need to develop new and exciting programs in order to be relevant to the community.

However, while the "new and exciting" can make the Church feel more relevant, in reality, it may still be out of touch with the real needs. For example, hunger does not require a creative and exciting response; it requires the offer of food. Loneliness requires inclusion; isolation requires community.

The Church can become lost in a world that defines competition in terms of becoming bigger, better and louder. But the character of the Church is in hearing the cry of the lost sheep and intently searching for that one lost coin.

To be a missional leader is sometimes more straightforward than we think. In its simplest form, to be missional is to equip the Church to hear the voice ignored by others. To be missional is to ask the question: "Is there something wrong?" That is an extremely relevant question for the children of God to ask, because we know that God's intent is to make things right.

—W.M.

▲   ▲   ▲

One day, the phone rang in Judy Paulsen's church office. It was one of the oldest members of the parish on the line, troubled by a story he had heard at his Kiwanis meeting. A staff person from a local school had called the home of an absent child to find out why she wasn't in class. The little girl replied: "My mommy has the coat."

Judy is rector of Christ Church, an Anglican parish in Oshawa, one of Ontario's motor cities whose fortunes rise and fall with companies like General Motors. And it's been in a bit of a free fall lately. But it was what the parishioner said next that encouraged Judy: "We oughta do something at Mary Street Community School."

The parishioner asked if Judy could send someone from the church's mission and outreach team down to the school to see how the church could help. "There was so much right about that transaction," says Judy. "He got it that we should get involved."

So, Christ Church is doing just that. Frances Thompson, a member of the outreach team, visited with the principal at the school to discover what their challenges are and how a local church could help. After the school got over its surprise that a church cared about their issues and was offering assistance, Fran discovered that Mary Street had students who can't afford to go on a field trip or buy a uniform for gym. That meeting was the beginning of the latest new relationship in Christ Church's missional journey.

Judy describes Fran and the rest of the outreach team as connectors—people who are entering the community and meeting with schools and groups to introduce themselves and Christ Church. They have two main goals: Ask and listen.

"We're guilty of saying to the world and our communities, 'Why can't you just take what we offer?'" says Judy, instead of finding out what they need. "And we have this wonderful tendency to ignore the fact that the Church is irrelevant to a lot of people."

For Fran, the evolution of outreach has been about saying, "Yes, there is a community and we can connect with things. The Church needs to be a comfort. I think you always need to be there for people. And word travels that the church is approachable. Maybe it's like a rebirth," says Fran.

The evolution of the mission and outreach team at Christ Church has gradually moved them from the sometimes easier, and still important task, of divvying up a budget for missions into a more direct connection with people in their community. When the idea of mission work changes from something that is seen as a long-distance phone call away, to a way of life that happens right outside your church's doorstep, a different kind of committee is required.

"We've started to ask different questions," explains Judy, who is on her own learning journey pursuing a Doctor of Ministry in Missional Leadership at Fuller Theological Seminary in Pasadena. "Instead of asking how we can attract people here, and how can we tend to the body of the congregation better, we've started to ask questions like 'What kind of community would we need to be so that God's love for the world can be known?' which is a very different kind of question. What are the relationships God wants us to develop in our community and the world so God's justice and peace can flourish? And how can we share the story of Jesus with people who haven't heard?"

For far too long, the Church has seen its job as feeding its people, but, says Judy, "we've gotten stuck in the feeding zone."

Some of the answers are simple. When a Christ Church connector visited a local high school, they learned there were kids who routinely missed classes because they simply could not afford bus passes, even at the reduced rate offered by the school of $47 per month. They plunked an empty peanut jar in front of the altar, called the campaign Tickets for Teens, and asked parishioners to donate.

"Our gift allowed the school to offer the passes for $20 a month instead. It was just one of those practical ways that the church can be seen as caring about the neighbourhood," says Judy. "When a guidance counsellor and a principal knows the church cares, then the staff knows and the parents know."

The team discovered that school supplies were an issue for some of the kids, so they filled backpacks and delivered them to the school.

"We heard back from the principal that the kids loved that the contents and the backpacks were all different," says Judy. "These things are so simple to do."

Ministries within Oshawa, like Gate 3:16, a drop-in for the homeless, and The Refuge, a youth outreach centre, used to receive cheques or supplies from Christ Church. Today, they also receive a visit from someone in Outreach to find out what's up and what's needed.

"When you have an actual relationship with people, then they can tell you what they really need. And it's a great encouragement to us. It's a two-way street, it enriches us," says Judy. The church recently did a drive for travel-sized shampoos and soaps. Those little bottles that travellers scoop up from hotel washrooms are the perfect size for people in shelters. Another member of the outreach team was involved in the Durham Aids Committee and knew that the organization needed furniture for their new facilities. Christ Church furnished the room the group uses to meet with families of people living with HIV and AIDS.

"This type of activity fits in with the missional question 'What is God already up to in our neighbourhood, our city and our world? And where would God like us to join in?'" says Judy. "There are tons of things already happening with people who have a heart for the marginal."

Christ Church is retraining themselves to do those two most basic of activities: Ask and listen.

Asking one particular question led Christ Church to launch Messy Church, one of their most chaotic of missional activities. A couple had their baby baptized at Christ Church, and then reappeared only when baby number two came along. As they met for baptism preparation, Judy asked them, "Why have we not been able to better connect with you?"

The couple replied that they just could not do Sunday mornings. They drop their kids off at daycare during the week and they did not want to be separated from them again on Sunday mornings—which were too rushed and frenzied when they did try to make it to church.

Christ Church answered with Messy Church (www.messychurch.org), a UK-born idea that offers a fun, loosey-goosey church experience for whole families one Saturday morning a month. There are crafts, songs, and Bible stories directed—at least within Christ Church's experiment—to the two- to six-year-old crowd and their parents or grandparents.

"Messy Church came out of this missional thinking of 'Ask, then listen.' And it's not ideal. How do you disciple someone when you only see them 10 times a year? But we didn't know their kids' names before—and now we do. We didn't know what was happening in their lives before— and now we know. We've found that the more relaxed and chaotic environment somehow helps us get better connected," explains Judy. Messy Church opens Christ Church's doors to a part of the community that feel they can't do Sunday mornings—but there is a time and a place for them at this particular church.

Christ Church is transforming back into the idea of an actual parish—a neighbourhood church that exists for the people, places and issues that surround it. "Sometimes, we get the idea that you have to be big to make a difference. I don't buy that," says Judy. "Mega-churches normally set up in warehouses in areas zoned for businesses. That itself can be a problem. I'm a big supporter of neighbourhood churches. There's a lot of potential for the neighbourhood church, if they ever came to life."

In Christ Church's own planning, they drew a two-kilometre circle around their church building on a map, and it is in that geographical area that their connectors focus their energy. It is an area that encompasses beautiful century homes as well as row-housing that has seen better days and where students used to be able to afford a field trip or a bus ticket.

Troy Pulchinski is a member of Christ Church's Missional Guide Team. The team has been meeting for about a year, and their main goal is to disseminate missional thinking throughout everything the church does. Is the budget missional? Is the worship missional? How do small groups reflect missional thinking?

"It's about having our church move towards really being a member of the community, so that when the question gets asked, 'If the church disappeared, would anyone care?' the answer would be yes," says Troy. "We want the answer to be that this group of people became a huge part of the community, and that their goal was never to fill pews, but to make a difference in the community in which we live."

The Missional Guide Team is behind a challenge issued to the entire congregation, to take the "ask and listen" approach to a whole new level—the frightening, personal one. The congregation has been asked to go and speak to non-church attending friends, neighbours or co-workers—anyone willing to talk. It is a six-week project presented in Christ Church's bulletin as an opportunity to "take our missional call as a church to a more personal level, by engaging with those around us in conversations about how our church might address hopes, dreams and questions they have."

Parishioners are encouraged to ask the people they speak with about their hopes and dreams for their neighbourhood and city; how a local community of faith might be able to encourage them; what would make them want, or not want, to explore a local church; and their questions and ideas related to faith or spirituality.

Then, the entire church is invited for a Saturday gathering to share and discuss what they heard and learned. It's a bit of a covert operation to get parishioners out in the community, and then shape some of Christ Church's future outreach activities, says Troy.

"We tend to over-think what being a missional church is, but sometimes it's just taking those little steps in a forward direction and being part of the community and letting people know that we're not so weird and different after all. I'm hoping," says Troy, "that our biggest problem will be deciding what not to do."

SOME OF WHAT THEY LEARNED ALONG THE WAY

- **Don't be afraid to redefine.** Judy's definition of missional has broadened to include the renewing of the whole parish, and she is seeing that come to life at Christ Church. "It is a parish that is what the church should be, a people called to be a blessing to the world that God loves."

- **Take the first step, however difficult.** Sometimes, those first meetings between connectors and community can be awkward. A nearby high school couldn't think of a way the church could help until Christ Church asked specifically about school supplies. A repeat visit, and a more gradual building of relationship might be required and appropriate.

- **Meet felt needs.** The projects that were "the most invigorating" have been the ones when a practical need was presented, and then quickly met. Those quick collections of towels for local shelters, socks for the homeless, a scooter for a disabled man in the area, lunches for a Habitat for Humanity crew, toothpaste—whatever—can help build up the missional muscles of a church just starting out on the journey.

- **Listen to your congregation.** Make your missional conversation broad and encompassing of the whole church. "The answer to what God wants us to do," says Judy, "actually resides among the people in the Sprit of God. You need to have this broad congregational discussion." In other words, ask and listen within your own context as well.

MISSIONAL DISCUSSION

1. Who are the voices in your community you believe you should be listening to?
2. How could your church's outreach and mission group evolve to become connectors?
3. What could happen in your congregation and community, if the entire body got involved in asking, listening and then sharing what it means to be missional?

CHAPTER NINE
Inclusive

St. Paul's Leaskdale

Leaskdale, Ont.

www.saintpauls.ca

AVERAGE WEEKLY ATTENDANCE: 650
DENOMINATIONAL AFFILIATION: Presbyterian
YEAR FOUNDED: 1862

It is an all too common assumption that God only works through the Church. Being missional challenges that assumption and that can be disconcerting. The missional approach defines God as constantly active—preferably through the Church, but certainly not limited to it.

The missional community recognises that whenever someone expresses that deep yearning for more, it is evidence of the activity of God. God is actively uncovering the divine image in all of us. And this activity can take place outside of church programs. In the old school, you are either in the Church or you are out. And if you are outside the Church, some simply assume that means you are apart from the activity of God.

The truly missional community is ready to risk the challenge of this commonly held notion, and to begin to entertain the thought that even those outside of the Church are contexts of God's activity. How do we align ourselves with this activity of God, rather than assume God's absence and potentially disregard the lives where God is surely at work?

When a church taps into this out-of-the-safety-of-the-box activity of God, they may discover unique opportunities for their members to express love to others. In doing so, they create an environment for people to discover that God loves them deeply.

—W.M.

▲   ▲   ▲

When a Canadian church gets involved with a short-term mission trip, our most dependable Christian worker-bees tend to be plunked into the available seats on the plane. Who can lead Bible drills *and* ask where the bathroom is in Spanish? Which middle-aged Canadian among us can build a roof in the blazing, tropical sun and not have a heart attack?

The idea of taking people on a missions trip who would likely break out into a cold sweat touring a Missions-Fest conference is a new thought for most congregations. But that's exactly what St. Paul's Presbyterian Church in

Leaskdale, Ont., did when they visited Hainamosa, Dominican Republic in the summer of 2008.

The Cantico Nuevo/Joyas de Cristo School in Hainamosa is familiar territory for St. Paul's. They have visited it before on short-term mission trips and support the work of the school and its outreach to the children of this neglected barrio. The neighbourhood was carved out of a sugar cane field years ago when the Dominican government relocated families from their homes to clear the way for a giant, concrete cross-shaped monument to Christopher Columbus. It was supposed to be a breathtaking, illuminated cross shining in the night sky, but, as it turns out, it's pricey to light up a 45-foot cross and electricity isn't always available anyway. Hainamosa was also supposed to have things like schools and medical clinics for the children and families who live there, but that has been slow to happen.

The summer missions trip in the Summer of 2008 was something different for St. Paul's. Nancy Loraine is director of missions at this church. With around 600 members or so, St. Paul's is at least three times the population of the hamlet connected to its name. The church is built in the middle of 100 acres of field and forest (just turn right after you pass Fresh Rooster's Fries). When the congregation began bursting out of its pews, they had to leave behind their quaint country church setting and build their new home around the corner. The old church is now an official landmark to Lucy Maud Montgomery who was the pastor's wife there half a lifetime ago.

The church has lent some of its surrounding land to the Canadian Foodgrains Bank to grow food for the world's hungry. Farmers who attend the church manage the project, planting and harvesting the produce that is sent around the world. Local businesses kick in the seeds and supplies. Church property also plays host to the Garden of Eatin', a communal plot for an agency that serves the homeless in the Durham region of this part of Ontario.

Nancy simmers with energy, almost to the point of a slow boil. She carries a photocopy of her favourite quote from the martyred Archbishop Oscar Romero around with her, and is quick to give a copy away. It reminds the Church that if it would "wish to incarnate within itself the sorrow, hope and anguish, of all who suffer and rejoice, that Church would be Christ loved and awaited, *Christ present*. And that depends on us."

Nancy talks about "being Christ present" and having a spirit that is "agile but not slippery, postured to move wherever God is leading you, being firm but not rigid. And responding deeply."

It was a deep response that was required when Nancy's neighbour Lydia pitched her an idea. Lydia, a photographer, had been intrigued by the Academy Award-winning documentary *Born into Brothels*, chronicling the life of children living in the red light district of Calcutta. The children were given cameras and asked to capture images of their world as they saw it.

Lydia wanted to travel overseas, put digital cameras into the hands of children in need, give them assignments and see how they and their world could change because of it. She knew more than a few people who were interested in going—all of them artsy, capable and enthusiastic—and none of them church-goers. What they needed was a struc-ture to hook the idea into and give it shape, direction and funding.

"Everyone who came up in the conversation were not at all affiliated with any congregation, but had a caring spirit for people and a love of art as a medium for expression and empowering people," explains Nancy. "For me, it's about how we can be Christ in the world. It's not about having this criteria that *unless* you are 'this,' we can't move for-ward, but rather, *because* you are 'this' I have this heart for you to know the Christ I know."

Nancy and the other leaders at St. Paul's thought of their friend Phyllis Novak, who runs a Toronto art studio for street youth. Sketch is not your typical Christian mis-sion. Its downtown location provides space for youth, aged 15 to 29 years old, to create art that helps them connect to themselves, each other, the community, and their own goals and dreams. After all, art heals in a way that other things can't. St. Paul's is among Sketch's supporters.

"Sketch is quite missional in and of itself, but we defi-nitely don't identify as such," says Phyllis. "However, we connected with the congregation's desire to be involved with something close to home that had young people at-tached to it and was innovative."

She was asked to join the photography-with-a-mission trip that was slowly taking shape out of St. Paul's. The idea expanded to include four youth who had come up—from some form of being street-involved—through the art trenches at Sketch.

"We underwrote the chance for these youth to go on the trip," says Andrew Allison, St. Paul's head pastor. "These kids were just at home and made neat connections. I don't know if anybody came to faith in Jesus Christ, but it felt a little gospel to us, that our resources would get spent on something that didn't benefit us. It sounds crazy enough to be the gospel."

The pastor that St. Paul's works with in Hainamosa was alerted to the fact that this particular St. Paul's trip was not mission as usual. "We knew," says Nancy, "that there was potential for drug use or alcohol abuse. Before they could leave the country, there were issues that one or two of the youth had to resolve before the courts."

Nothing very bad happened. In fact, a lot of *very good* happened. Forty-eight Dominican kids learned photographic skills and some of their shots have been displayed in Canadian studios and copies sold to create a scholarship fund for them back home.

"Every single person who went on the team got a great opportunity to assess who they were, figure out where they wanted to go from there and see something very different," says Phyllis. "These guys would not have had this opportunity. It affected our lives quite a bit, and we just had a lovely time. There was music, art-making, photography and a general sense of joy."

For St. Paul's, the idea of sending street kids on a mission trip fits into the vibe they strive to create in their own church community. Their understanding of missional—at this stage of their church life—is rooted in an authenticity about not having it all together and an acknowledgement of both the brokenness and potential of everyone who walks through the front door.

"Sometimes, there's the sense that you need to clean yourself up before you come to church," says Andrew. "But the conversations aren't neat and tidy like we used to imagine ourselves to be. We are out in the sticks, we're in the middle of nowhere. Something is happening here that people feel they can fit, even if they aren't 'in the club.'"

Part of St. Paul's approach to making people comfortable being just who they are, where they are, means being fluid around all the edges, including in the service. "We are not form looking for life," says Andrew. "We are life looking for form." Chairs can be shifted around for circles of sharing, art can happen in the middle, sightings of clerical collars are rare, and when it comes time for communion, Andrew offers the bread to whoever would like to serve that day. Kids come running.

Andrew's preaching style includes disclosure of what he considers his own personal failures. It's okay, he says, to be known in part by your former reputation if it is "almost like a badge of honour: This is what Jesus rescued me from." Transparency from the person standing at the front of the church enables people sitting in the middle to be honest that they do not have it all together—that they have made big, thrashing nightmares of mistakes too and can live through telling the tale, having been released and restored.

Yes, St. Paul's Leaskdale has a growing portfolio of outreach ministries. But being missional is mostly a mood there these days. St. Paul's has history and yet it's hip—out on the edges, but still strong in the centre. Like many changing, growing, missional-minded congregations, it is a church finding its way.

"Our 'go and tell' piece has yet to be written," says Andrew. "We don't exactly have a prostitution problem in Leaskdale, but within earshot, marriages are crumbling. And a Christian who is fully alive, willing to be vulnerable and grace-filled, they—and not a program—are the best thing going."

SOME OF WHAT THEY LEARNED ALONG THE WAY

- **Great ideas can come from unexpected places.** The idea for the photography trip did not come from within the congregation, but from someone who trusted it.
- **Let go of the old and dream big.** When the congregation of St. Paul's decided to sell their historic building and construct a new, much larger facility, their mindset was to build it for their community, not for themselves. That focus helped centre the vision and the decisions that needed to be made throughout the entire process.
- **Risks are real.** The church knew that to send Toronto street youth to a developing country on a mission trip might be inviting problems—for the kids, the hosts, the church. They took careful steps to protect everyone who was participating at every step along the way.

- **It is easy to become discouraged.** "Too many of my pastor friends (and pastors I know about) have become discouraged and disillusioned, leaving for something that might hold more promise. I believe that missional is sacrificial, slow, steady, long-term commitment with a whole different measure of success," says Sharon Simmonds, interim administrative pastor at Leaskdale.

MISSIONAL DISCUSSION

1. Is there a risky missional opportunity—like sending un-churched youth on a church-sponsored trip—that your church could take?
2. How could increased transparency in preaching add to the missional growth of your congregation?
3. What is your reaction to "we are not form looking for life, but life looking for form?"

CHAPTER TEN
Activists

Southridge Community Church
_____

St. Catharines, Ont.

www.southridgechurch.ca

AVERAGE WEEKLY ATTENDANCE: 1,500

DENOMINATIONAL AFFILIATION: Mennonite Brethren

YEAR FOUNDED: 1980, relocated 2003

If we are serious about running towards God, we will find ourselves running towards the marginalized and disenfranchised. Because that is what God does. God intentionally searches out those in need and sprints toward them. To be aligned with God is to run in that same direction. Missional congregations seek to join in where God is at work.

To intentionally relocate to the centre of need is no small task. Often, those are exactly the kinds of places that we try our best to avoid.

Not necessarily out of ill will, but because of a natural tendency to
avoid discomfort. We would love to express our concern in a safe and
perhaps more distant fashion.

But imagine what it would be like to move intentionally towards
the homeless? Imagine what it would be like to stand in solidarity with
the weak and to embrace the rejected. To engage in this imaginative
intentionality is to discover the real presence and activity of God.
Once you see that, you will never look back.

—W.M.

A   A   A

At first glance, Doug and Cate have little in common.
Doug is a man of the streets, or at least he used to
be. His voice is raspy, worn, but thoughtful. You
can tell he's lived "a hard life," as people say, and the tat-
tooed teardrop on his cheek hints at stories not lightly
shared. But he found his way off the streets and into the life
of Southridge Community Church in St. Catharines, Ont.
He lived in their shelter for the homeless off and on for four
years. Doug still hangs out there on a regular basis.

"I found God here. This place is good. I came here to get
to know God, and I found Him. When I first came here, I
was homeless," says Doug. "It's not my plan to live on the
streets again. I'll always have a home."

Cate is articulate and polished—with a pleasing touch
of funky. She's never even come close to being homeless
and found success in her career as a pharmaceutical sales
representative. But her work left her empty and unfulfilled,

a story that has repeated itself so many times you'd think we would all finally know better.

"I was spinning my wheels, there was always something wrong, inner turmoil, not knowing how to fix this or heal that. Then, I walked into this place and saw people living lives in ways and behaving in ways and feeling in ways that I think I was longing for," says Cate.

She started off as a volunteer at the front desk of the "hotel for Jesus" that Southridge runs. Something about the work she was doing and the people like Doug that she was meeting touched her in a deep place and made her re-evaluate everything in her life. Cate and her husband are now preparing their family for her transition from corporate to compassion—she is entering into full-time service at Southridge.

Everything has changed for Cate—her marriage, how she views her children and herself, her entire life. "Once you experience this environment, and that kind of healing, it's impossible to go back," says Cate, beginning to cry. "I feel a calling here, and my life is nothing like it was."

It is important to know that the homeless shelter Southridge runs, where Doug and Cate both started new lives, is not down the road from the church. It's down the hallway. About six years ago, the congregation moved from their pretty little church in the country to a vacant school building in the heart of St. Catharines, all in an attempt to be missional. Sunday school classrooms, administrative offices, meeting rooms, the sanctuary where the church worships and a homeless shelter—they all share the same roof and the same wide hallways that used to house children dashing from class to class.

"We were a small but growing church in rural St. Catharines, with grapevines all over us, but nowhere near people with real needs," explains lead pastor Jeff Lockyer. "We realized that for us to really be a missional community required some proximity to people, let alone the marginalized. We were trying to become missional, but were convicted that to have the lifestyle we were trying to live, we couldn't live out in the boonies," says Jeff.

Instead of expanding their facility, the church sold their property and bought the school, one mile from downtown St. Catharines. Southridge quickly connected with an Out of the Cold program, where churches work together to serve the homeless to one degree or another, which eventually led to the construction of a 36-bed hostel in their renovated building, open 24/7, with a big, stainless steel kitchen that serves up three hot meals a day. The church also offers well-used space to social service agencies that meet with clients right there, on the spot.

The church itself grew to its current size of about 1,500 people, many of them intrigued by the idea of a church that includes a shelter for the homeless and endless opportunities to serve the poor and marginalized in their own church building. There is a genuine attempt to build authentic community at Southridge, where those who are apparently whole, like Cate, come face to face with the so-obviously broken, like Doug—and realize they may actually need to be rearranged and put back together again themselves.

Tim Arnold is outreach pastor for Southridge: "We have a pretty unapologetic message that there is a side to us that will never be realized unless we are in relationship with the poor and the marginalized, beyond token serving projects once a year."

Jeff says the church, in its missional move and all that has followed, has "tried to aggressively redefine the invitation of faith we are giving people, with the homeless initiatives, our brand, our reputation in the community... this is an agent to serve our region. This is us serving people, not an entity *for* us."

There seems to be a spiritual win/win going on here. The poor are served and see Jesus in the faces of the women and men spending time with them. And the ordinary, sometimes unsuspecting volunteers like Cate who wander through the doors to spend time at the shelter, discover Jesus in the faces and stories of those they serve. And everyone has the potential to have their lives and faith be transformed because of it. The pastors here believe with all their hearts that when we serve, we grow. Spiritual growth accelerates as people dive outside of their comfort zones and into arenas like the homeless shelter down the hall.

Jeff goes by the example in Luke 8 and 9, where Jesus has done a fair bit of teaching, and you'd think the disciples would be starting to catch on. "Then, he's calming the seas and they are looking at Him and saying, 'Who is this guy?' Even Jesus only produced a 'Who is this man?' level of faith. But all of a sudden, He empowers them to go out there and heal the sick and be amongst the poor. They come back, and they know who He is. They get it."

They do, and it is then that they understand. South-ridge's leaders have seen the Cate-Doug dynamic play out countless times. It did in Tim's own life, before he was out-reach pastor and volunteering at the shelter. "It taught me about my brokenness," he shares. "It gets you in touch with this level of judgementalism, pride, a massive blockage to experiencing Christ and living out my real calling that I didn't even know was there.

"In the ongoing connection between call and duty, there is a lot of duty in the New Testament to change the world around us. We can easily push people out of duty, but the flip side of duty is calling. Without being in rela-tionship with the needy, the poor, the marginalized, we are just not going to be what God has designed us to be," says Tim.

This discipleship boot camp doesn't only happen within Southridge's walls. The church also organizes disci-pleship trips to places like Guatemala, Jamaica and New Orleans. The trips are designed, according to Southridge's newsletter, "as an experiential learning tool to expose you to another culture, meet some basic needs in that commu-nity, and challenge you in your own faith journey as you grow as a Christ follower."

But it is back here at home where Southridge is making missional milestones, including with social service agencies in the Niagara region who have not seen anything quite like this church before.

Brian Hutchings is commissioner of community ser-vices for Niagara region, who is in charge of everything from nursing homes to work programs to homeless programs. The tagline for his department is "Building Communities. Building Lives." He sees how Southridge, who he calls "a valuable community partner," does both.

Southridge's leadership met with Brian way back at the beginning when they first made their move closer to downtown, and told him they wanted to stand in the gap in the Niagara region. They asked him what was needed, and how they could help. Part of Southridge's plan was to be a church connected with an anchor cause. They met with Brian and other community groups already at work in the community to determine what that cause should be.

"Out of the blue, they offered to build a homeless shelter, if that's what was needed. But they went beyond that. They said that instead of people just sleeping overnight and sending them on their way, they were going to give them pyjamas to sleep in and wash their clothes for them at night, so the next day they leave clean," says Brian. "They told me they were going to connect the people who came to the shelter with people in their congregation as mentors, and to help them get on their feet. They started engaging with these guys who were disengaged."

Brian explains that if you put a homeless guy in a mansion, they're just going to be homeless again. "You need somebody to walk with you," says Brian.

Which is exactly the path that Southridge is walking down. "The missing ingredient in marginalized people groups is ongoing relationships," says Jeff. "The government has all kinds of programs, but they need the relational support to build them up to access the support. Only the Church can offer the hands and feet. Only the Church can really give a crap about these people," says Jeff. "It's not so much that they are homeless, but that they are relationless. We got into this to create ongoing, authentic relationships so we could really make a difference in this marginalized people group."

When Brian Hutchings travels around the province, he uses the Southridge shelter story as a model to demonstrate how a faith community can be a vital partner in serving the homeless. Recently, Southridge had another of those out-of-the-blue conversations with Brian, when they told him they were expanding to a multi-site model in nearby Welland and North St. Catharines. They asked him what the gaps were in those areas, and how they could bridge them. The identified issues—sole-support parents and marginalized seniors—are the anchor causes for the two newest Southridge sites of worship.

"Ultimately, the locations will rally around a compassion, justice issue," explains Tim. "They will attempt to meet needs that are unmet needs in those areas. When we moved here, we didn't start a shelter right away, we started partnering with a bunch of agencies. Strategically, we are launching these sites with a partnership model. We are having conversations and connecting with partners that are all doing great work in that area and in relational-based ways. Our expectation is that there is no shortage of need, and a specific role for Southridge to play. We don't know what that is yet."

But it will almost certainly involve people like Doug and Cate who appear to be very different, at least on the surface.

SOME OF WHAT THEY LEARNED ALONG THE WAY

- **Partner with others who are already on track.** Southridge met with municipal and provincial agencies, and asked how they could help. They partnered with the agencies all along the way, including providing free office space to enable them to meet with the men and women who are staying at the shelter.

- **Relationships are the foundation.** Southridge's leaders were prayerful about what they could offer that was missing from the chain of support given to the homeless. They realized it was the ongoing, dependable relationships that could eventually empower people in need to access the government-run supports already in place.

- **Equip and motivate the members.** Southridge provides multiple "on-ramps" that congregation members can travel to be engaged in service projects. They include one-hour orientation sessions to the homeless shelter, offered on a regular basis. The church also hosts an annual "GO" conference to encourage members who may agree with the lifestyle of serving, in theory, but lack the confidence to be engaged. The conference focuses on motivating, equipping and mobilizing the community for action.

- **Find, and give, support.** Southridge has been involved in Willow Creek's Leadership Summit, and more recently a pilot project called Leader's Village that focuses on mentoring among like-minded leaders. The "coaching clusters" help iron sharpen iron.

MISSIONAL DISCUSSION

1. Who are the marginalized in your community?
2. Jeff believes that "there is a side to us that will never be realized unless we are in relationship with the poor and the marginalized, beyond token serving projects once a year." How could you lead your congregation towards greater engagement with the poor?
3. Southridge believes strongly in coming alongside partners, including secular agencies, already at work in the community. What would be the advantages and disadvantages of that approach for your church?

CHAPTER ELEVEN
Responders

Nouvelle Vie

Montreal, Que.

www.nouvellevie.com

AVERAGE WEEKLY ATTENDANCE: 3,500

DENOMINATIONAL AFFILIATION: ACF Association
   Chrétienne pour la francophonie

YEAR FOUNDED: 1993

When we want to discover what God is doing in a given community, a good place to start is to consider what God is able to do. With that as the starting point, the sky is the limit. This kind of holy confidence can enable churches to dream, to plan, to respond—even with a moment's notice—to the prompting of God to reach out into their communities.

Typically, we ask God to align with our work, but becoming missional means we align with what God is doing. We can expect, there-

fore, God-type resources, ideas and opportunities that are larger than ourselves. But God always comes prepared.

Isaiah 58 is an excellent text for considering the missional journey. It speaks of the wonderful imagery of God's response to our faithful risk-taking: "Light will break forth as the dawn; we will be like a well watered garden and a spring that never fails."

But this beautiful imagery follows an exhaustive response of the people of God in caring for the poor, clothing the naked and securing justice for others. God acts, we respond. We act in applying grace, and God responds.

Sometimes our responses aren't even planned. All across Canada, there are times when churches are simply doing what needs to be done—at the very moment it needs to be done. Harsh situations in particular—like the extremes of our Canadian climate—sometimes require immediate response. When finding a stranded motorist on a freezing winter night, the required response is obvious. There's no time or need to call a committee meeting.

The congregation that has confidence in God's rich resources is ready to be aligned with God's extravagant activity of grace. And if a congregation is ready to be aligned with God's extravagant activity of grace—then they need to be prepared for one exciting ride. Because when responding with God, the sky really is the limit.

—W.M.

⚔   ⚔   ⚔

The term "triangle of darkness" may sound dramatic now, but in the early days of January 1998, it fit the situation perfectly. Canada's worst ever ice storm gripped large sections of Ontario, Quebec and New Brunswick. Roads were treacherous, electricity was gone for weeks in some communities and tree branches wore thick, icy armour that were lethal weapons when they cracked and fell.

No area was harder hit by the hours of freezing rain than Montreal's South Shore. That is where the communities in that geographic triangle of Canada's worst weather disaster yet struggled to meet the needs of their citizens and reassure ordinary Canadians—who know better than anyone what winter is—that they would live through this one. The lights and the heat would come back on, eventually.

One church in the community of Longueuil on the South Shore marks the ice storm as a turning point in becoming an active, missional presence in their community. Nouvelle Vie is a protestant, evangelical church in a society that, even though many may dismiss it over coffee as irrelevant to their lives, is still shaped, steeped and defined by a deep connection to the Roman Catholic Church.

In a society like Quebec's, a church like theirs may be viewed as cultish and suspicious, or just plain weird. Some reports claim there are fewer evangelical Christians in Quebec than in Cuba. Christians of this persuasion may scramble for a foothold for years before finding their way in their communities, and being considered a welcome equal.

Which makes Nouvelle Vie's success at missional living all the more remarkable.

"During the ice storm of 1998," recalls assistant pastor Jocelyn Olivier, "the church was one of the only buildings in the city with power because we had a generator. The city officers discovered the church and we became partners for days and weeks."

Nouvelle Vie opened its doors to hundreds of families as a shelter, even cancelling Sunday services because the sanctuary was full of people in sleeping bags, surrounded by their suitcases and knapsacks stacked around them. Five hundred families lived in the church for up to three weeks.

"From there, we began a very good relationship with the city of Longueuil. Everyone in the city started to know who we were. It really helped to break down the walls," says Jocelyn. "It was God's moment, even through the storm."

Suzanne Fournier is general director of Action Nouvelle Vie, the centre that offers "tangible assistance to families and individuals who are struggling with poverty." It is the outreach arm of the church, but technically a separate entity. This is an important distinction in Quebec and removes some barriers for the community who might be initially reluctant to tap into a church ministry.

"We have worked really hard with the community to build a strong, trust relationship. We are slowly and surely getting there," says Suzanne.

Suzanne says that Nouvelle Vie was "the 911 of the city during the ice storm. We had started our outreach work before, but it was much smaller then. We were helping some families, but the ice storm put us on the map."

It's an odd way to get a missional break, and Suzanne laughs when she describes it as that. "It's funny how things work. We didn't even stop to think during the ice storm that it would have that good of an impact in the community. We were just occupied with meeting an urgent need."

A few months after the storm, Nouvelle Vie invited the mayor to drop by and they honoured him during a service for his efforts during the ice storm. Today, the city often refers families in crisis to Nouvelle Vie, confident that they will receive the help they need.

Suzanne says that Action Nouvelle Vie reaches out to 8,000 people each month, to varying degrees, through the different programs they offer. Many of them are immigrants. Each year, Quebec welcomes an average of 45,000 immigrants who come from over 100 countries. They find themselves struggling to stay afloat "like a dot in the ocean," says Marie-Elise Perreault, communications officer for Action Nouvelle Vie. The workers at Action Nouvelle Vie's food bank had begun to notice that more than half of those coming regularly for help were immigrants.

"When we realized their needs were greater than just giving food and clothing, we wanted to develop a program especially for them. Immigrants faced three big challenges. Language is one; a lack of social networks was another; and they have a very hard time getting into the marketplace for work," says Marie-Elise.

Action Nouvelle Vie decided to build a program based on the needs they had identified to empower immigrants to tackle these barriers and "help them be autonomous for their well-being and for their kids," says Marie-Elise. World Vision Canada, more commonly associated with international development work, became their partner.

Nick Azzuolo is World Vision Canada's Quebec guy. "World Vision was doing more direct work in Canada," explains Nick, "We decided to partner with existing organizations and build capacity with groups already on the ground. We decided to collaborate—instead of compete—and share the expertise we have gained in years of international development."

When World Vision first started searching for Canadian partners to work with, they thought of Christian non-government organizations (NGOs) first. But as more and more Canadian churches go missional, World Vision finds itself working with churches who want to tap into their expertise and ability to offer funding to programs which they believe to have missional potential.

"We've come alongside Nouvelle Vie and trained them on how to do transformational development, helping them to take it a step further," says Nick.

Translate Hope is one of the flagship programs Nouvelle Vie offers to immigrants, with the goal of helping new Canadians integrate better into Quebecois society. Immigrants practice French and participate in cultural activities like the infamous Quebec maple sugar shack, so they can better understand the unique world they have stepped into. They also gain access to things like job training to speed up their transition into the workplace.

"World Vision has given us great tools in the growth of our organization," says Suzanne. "Now if we want to start a program, we do a community assessment first. We gather everyone together, including all the different stakeholders, and inform them of our intent. We see what's being done because we want to see that we are meeting a real need in our community. If the need is there and it fits with our values and if we have the resources we need to get started—and sometimes we don't at first—we rely on our faith and believe that God will open the doors and the resources will come."

Part of the value that World Vision has brought is a deeper understanding of what transformational development is, and how it is measured. "That means we're tracking the growth that happens through the programs," explains Nick. "If somebody wanted to learn how to jump, at the beginning, she only knows how to jump four feet. But at the end, she can jump five. We're tracking the growth that happens through the programs. What is the language proficiency of the participants after their language training?"

Those are the elements that churches often struggle with, says Nick. "Often we don't take the time to evaluate what we're doing. Is it making a difference? Sometimes, when you're doing crisis intervention, you're enabling the problem instead of solving it. If you have a mobile canteen going downtown giving out food to homeless people, are you enabling them to stay homeless?" Those are big questions. Nouvelle Vie is still working on the answers.

Good Start, a program aimed at young mothers and their children, is in the pilot stage with Nouvelle Vie, with World Vision acting again as partner, partial funder and cheerleader. Good Start helps young mothers struggling with poverty by providing support during the pregnancy and necessities like diapers, bottles and some clothing after the baby is born. Mothers come for a food basket each week. At the same time, they attend meetings to share and discuss topics close to their hearts. Volunteer grandmothers tend the babies while the mothers meet, providing them a much-needed break as well.

All of Nouvelle Vie's programs—which span the missional gamut from getting kids ready for school with new backpacks and reduced prices on new clothing and shoes, to a distribution of Christmas hampers the scope of which puts Santa to shame—start out with an idea that rises out of an observed need. Careful research determines if the program fits into Nouvelle Vie's mandate and if it can work. Then, there is a commitment to doing it well and with partners who may be already at work in the community.

"Nouvelle Vie has tremendous potential because they are able to draw on networks of support they have and there is a genuine desire to make a difference," observes Nick. "When a church shows a congregation they can make an impact on the community through transformational changes, it encourages the church to increase their potential."

It may also grow the church. Nouvelle Vie certainly has. In 1993 they numbered 75; today around 3,500. Assistant pastor Jocelyn believes there are two solid reasons for the steady and sustained growth of Nouvelle Vie. First of all, they do things well.

"From worship, to parking, to ushers, to nurseries, we share our heart for excellence for God. People were not afraid or shy to invite people to church. They are proud of what we offer. The church building itself is not a palace, but it's nice."

The second reason—and perhaps a more common one for missional church growth—finds its root in Isaiah 58, a favourite passage of Claude Houde, Nouvelle Vie's head pastor and popular international speaker. If there is a founding passage of Nouvelle Vie, this is the one.

It starts with God sending his children to their room for their—yet again—blatant disobedience. Then, "Is this not the kind of fasting I have chosen: to loose the chains of injustice and untie the cords of the yoke, to set the oppressed free and break every yoke? Is it not to share your food with the hungry and to provide the poor wanderer with shelter—when you see the naked to clothe him and not to turn away from your own flesh and blood?"

And then one of the most beautiful, life-giving passages ever: "*Then*, your light will break forth like the dawn, and your healing will quickly appear…you will be like a well-watered garden, like a spring whose waters never fail."

Being missional, says Jocelyn, quite simply, "pleases the heart of God." When we serve, "we are in the middle of the will of God. Isaiah 58 is the chapter that explains the vision of the church. Take care of the people who can't give back to you in return, and God will provide for you and take care of you by adding people to the church."

SOME OF WHAT THEY LEARNED ALONG THE WAY

- **Be ready and on-hand in a crisis.** In the wake of SARS, H1N1 and even ice storms that gripped the country, many Canadian churches have developed disaster plans. If your church does not have a disaster response plan, consider creating one.
- **Invite community leaders to church events.** Nouvelle Vie regularly includes the mayor and other municipal leaders in things that are going on at their church and outreach centre. The church is demystified and walls come down as people grow more comfortable.
- **Welcome volunteers from the community** who may not necessarily attend your church. This builds bridges and fosters good relationships, not to mention that those volunteers bring their own set of unique skills.
- **Focus on excellence.** "Because of Nouvelle Vie's desire to do things well, they are able to make progress within the community," commends Nick. "People's expectations today are for excellence. When the church demonstrates that, there is a greater response."

MISSIONAL DISCUSSION

1. How could your church prepare itself to respond during a natural disaster in your community?
2. Nick Assoulo notes that, "People's expectations today are for excellence." How strong is this value in your church?
3. How could a partnership with a like-minded organization resource your congregation in its missional work?

CHAPTER TWELVE
Presence

Main Street Baptist Church
Saint John, N.B.
www.mainstreetbaptist.ca

AVERAGE WEEKLY ATTENDANCE: 400
DENOMINATIONAL AFFILIATION: Baptist
YEAR FOUNDED: 1842

Most churches hope that by engaging with their immediate neighbour-hood, they will see people coming face to face with God. This is espe-cially true when in a context of obvious need. But not every congrega-tion finds itself in the midst of a low-income district or in an environ-ment where children feel threatened by gangs.

The beautiful thing about a missional approach is that it puts the focus on finding God, wherever you are. On the surface, that appears to be a fairly easy and routine task for the Church. If someone wants

to find God, going to a church would be a safe bet. The missional
church concept does not dispute this, but it expands on it.

If God is present everywhere, then God is active everywhere. That
means God is already *active in the neighbourhood. This is particu-*
larly true if the neighbourhood is experiencing fear, loneliness and
need. Where there is poverty, fear and need, there you will find the
presence and activity of God.

When the Church becomes aligned with the activity of God in that
neighbourhood—no matter how troubled it is—then the full intent of
God's activity can be realized. In fact, as a result, both *those outside*
and inside the church will come face to face with God.

—W.M.

▲   ▲   ▲

Main Street Baptist in Saint John, New Brunswick
was missional before missional was even cool. It
started as a church-plant way back in 1842 and
has since grown to become an essential entity in what is
now a rough-and-tumble Saint John neighbourhood
known as the Old North End.

If Main Street was a person, she would be the grand
matron in the old, sprawling house on the corner, who has
been there long enough that people know she really, truly
cares. She would be the *beautiful* one. Which is a word that
this church uses to describe what it wishes to be.

Beautiful as an adjective and a goal came up at a staff
retreat as four pastors sat around talking about values to

frame their congregation. "Our senior pastor came up with the phrase, 'Beautiful Church,' to describe what we wanted to be. It captures the idea of being a diverse fellowship, yet being one in Jesus Christ," explains John Knight, outreach pastor for Main Street. "We have people in our church who make less than $10,000 a year and we have people who make more than a million. We have white folks and immigrants, foreign students, and a wide range in ethnicity, socio-economics and age. We are this wonderful kaleidoscope of people who are all one in Jesus Christ. And that's beautiful."

The neighbourhood itself has seen better days. The Old North End is the part of town that some people avoid if they can. The streets that were once bustling and healthy because of industries like shipping are now depressed. For a time, drug dealers ruled. North End residents have an unemployment rate that is triple the rest of their city's (30.5 per cent); almost half of its households are managed by a single mother and the average household income is $28,000. Forty-one per cent of the population do not have a high school diploma. Crime rates are higher on these particular streets.

Some churches would have fled to the suburbs, but Main Street dug in its heels and kept doing what they have always done—and more. At the program level, Main Street offers many, but Hope Mission is a flagship. North End residents can drop in, have a coffee, enjoy a free hot lunch twice a week, choose items from a clothing bank and hear a spiritual talk. "The biggest need in this neighbourhood is a sense of spiritual belonging. Hope Mission is kind of a church within a church," explains John. "We are trying to see the people of the neighbourhood as family."

Prime Time is a Sunday afternoon "Sunday School for the neighbourhood" that has been meeting for over 25 years. "We have a couple of adult classes, including one for single mothers and kid classes. Then, we all have supper together."

John has noticed that the Main Street members who seem specifically called and particularly gifted to the Hope Mission and Prime Time ministries have often walked through some of life's thickest jungles themselves. "You would find among them," observes John, "an overabundance of the gift of mercy. These are people who have gone through tough stuff in their own lives, and God has gifted them with an ability to extend deep mercy to others."

Community had fallen apart in the Old North End, says John. "We are filling that void, and in the deepest sense, having people come face to face with God. That's the mission." Main Street is not alone in its mission on these streets. And they know that. They do not see themselves as the only one with answers, but they know theirs is unique.

As the neighbourhood deteriorated, concerned groups realized they had to work together to increase safety and improve life for the residents. Main Street was part of it from the beginning. Partnerships lie at the core of Main Street's missional presence in the Old North End. The most obvious example is The ONE (Old North End) Change community group that formed in 2004 to improve the quality of life in the area. A representative from one church sits on the board, and that is John. The church heard there was a group forming and invited them to use the church facilities to meet. A gesture as simple as that—opening up the church facilities and offering it for free to community groups to meet—has been a profound part of Main Street's identity in the neighbourhood.

In an age when the Church can be viewed as irrelevant, Main Street is seen as essential. "The ONE Change board welcomes the church's presence because of the church's reputation in this neighbourhood. It is a safe haven and the life-line. There is a sense that we have to be on this board. As you sit at the table, you gain respect. It's as easy as doing it. And it's amazing," says John.

Scott Crawford is chair of The ONE Change board, and a "not-a-big-church-person" kind of guy. "But I'm the biggest fan of Main Street Baptist. They have really given me a lot of new respect for what churches are capable of, and what they are all about," he says. For Scott, it has been refreshing to witness Main Street's programs effectively improving life for North End residents and to witness their willingness to work with other groups who share the same concerns. "To see a religious organization—and they certainly have a strong religious component to what they do—be so community-based, that everyone feels welcome. They have a fabulous group of caring people, but lots of churches have that. I think what makes it different is that they are about the community, not only their own congregation."

When Scott first started his stint as chair of the board, he wanted to meet people from the neighbourhood in their own homes. "I wanted to go door to door and meet people," says Scott. "John was the guy I called to see if he'd stroll around the neighbourhood with me. I knew they'd open the door for John. If Main Street says 'it's okay,' then it's okay."

For years, kids from a nearby school have been coming for lunch, fun and games at Main Street's Hope Mission. However, in the last couple of years, gang members intimidated them on their walk over. The kids stopped coming. Main Street talked about it with ONE Change, and volunteers now walk the kids over so they can have their free lunch and play time at the church. Youth crime is a huge issue in the neighbourhood, so community groups, including Main Street, joined forces to ensure that every night of the week, there is a youth activity offered in the Old North End.

When ONE Change wanted to offer a free health clinic, they were having a hard time getting people to come. "Main Street opened their arms and said they'd hold it before their lunch program," says Scott. "Immediately the numbers went through the roof, because people trust Main Street. They talk about that Christian ideal of helping others, and they truly live it."

Trust is based on both presence and action. When a proposal was made to close one of the public schools in the Old North End, Main Street wrote a letter to the District Education Council expressing their concern and outlining what such a school closure would do to an already struggling neighbourhood. Recognizing they have a voice, Main Street uses it.

Working with different secular community groups—with people of different faiths or no faith at all—to care for the orphan, the widow, the oppressed among them, "is still a radical idea in some circles," says John. "We are a solid, mainstream, evangelical church. And we see our primary task to share Jesus with the world. But Kingdom stuff is by definition whole-person stuff. And it is not just people in the Church who are doing this stuff. People are working to bring about change for people, and God is using them." John has seen credibility trump caricature by entering into partnerships willing to listen, and not willing to preach.

"I'm just myself. You go in and you be real. If you are genuinely receptive to ideas, if you talk intelligently about issues and concerns, then if they ever had a caricature in their minds of what a pastor is, or what a Christian is, they start to get past that." And of course, prejudice is a two-way street. "If I had a perception that the director of teen resources of some group is a wild and crazy guy who spends all his time talking about safe sex, as I spend time with him and get to know him, I understand that is not true."

Main Street does not see itself as separate from, holier than, or better than, the other concerned citizens they partner with. "We are seen as a genuine partner, that we really do have a stake in working with others where there is common ground," explains John. When you start working with other community partners, you find "people who are extraordinarily committed and dedicated and thoughtful. They may not speak the same language as you, but they are deeply committed. If we believe that God works in extraordinary ways, if we believe that God is ultimately in control of things, and working and shaping history to bring about God's Kingdom, then God is working in these situations too. These people who are working to bring about change for other people, God is using them," says John. The Church is stepping into what God already has going on in the neighbourhood. And God can use whoever God wants.

Going missional is about expanding God's Kingdom and not our church congregations. But both have grown at Main Street. It is a church bursting at the seams. They have outgrown their lovely, historic, crumbling kind-of-church at 211 Main Street and have launched a Greater Things campaign to move their congregation to a new, larger location about one kilometre away. For the community of the Old North End, one kilometre might as well be 100.

Except that Main Street Baptist is also staying on Main Street. They will use their old facility to increase the ministry opportunities in the Old North End. They believe that God has told them to pack up and stay.

"Our integrity rests in the fact that we are here. As we shift there [to the new location,] it opens up our property here, to think differently." Part of that "thinking differently," elaborates John, will include "addressing housing issues in this neighbourhood, through our partnerships."

As Main Street works through the meaning and implications of this move, the partnerships they have nurtured are proving to be key. "They are essential to the next step of the development of our ministry in this neighbourhood. Main Street's partners will benefit from the space available to them in the renovated, original building," says John. "We can look at things like moving the food bank in the neighbourhood into our revamped facility. Maybe we can change it to a cooperative food bank that empowers people. Maybe a playground, because right now there isn't one."

The ideas are limitless. "As they plan on moving into bigger digs, they still remain so committed to the neighbourhood that we don't feel like we're losing them," says Scott. "In fact, we feel like we're going to be gaining something."

SOME OF WHAT THEY LEARNED ALONG THE WAY

- **Adopt a posture of humility.** Main Street Baptist enters into partnerships with other community groups in a position of humility *and* strength. They don't believe they have all the best answers, but they believe they have a right and a responsibility to be at the table. They want to be there, and it shows. They are respected because of that.

- **Agree to disagree without being offensive.** Sitting in meetings and entering into partnerships with secular organizations, or even Christians of different persuasions, will mean that you don't always agree with every opinion offered, or issue discussed. "I've never avoided my faith," says John, "but I've also never been 'in your face.' You better be prepared to sit and listen. Hopefully, you're not always jumping in and saying, 'Well, the Bible says this and that.' You have to listen. The conversation has to be broad. Folks know where we stand. What we try to do is work constructively with people on things. It works."

- **Know your neighbourhood.** Something as simple as a visit to Statistics Canada's website can give you the facts about who is living in your neighbourhood, and information on things like income and education levels. Municipal studies are probably available locally to help you better understand your community's profile.

- **Ask the right questions.** "Here's your community, now what is our Biblical response?" is the question to be asked, says John. "Some things will focus specifically on their relationship with Jesus Christ. Some will focus on the challenges in their lives."

- **Think long-term.** "We have miles to go," says John. "To the extent that you are involved in these broader things, you are part of a generational solution. Some things aren't going to go away right away. You really have to take the long view."

MISSIONAL DISCUSSION

1. Who are the mercy-givers in your current church community that could be mobilized for ministry?
2. Does the thought of being involved in boards and committees outside of the more predictable church groups exhaust or excite you?
3. Name some of the challenges you might have to work through to overcome potential—and probably mutual—suspicion or distrust if your church reaches out to secular community groups and attempts to build partnerships. How would you overcome these challenges?

CHAPTER THIRTEEN
Bridge-builders

Faith Tabernacle

Halifax, N.S.

www.faithhalifax.org

AVERAGE WEEKLY ATTENDANCE: 300

DENOMINATIONAL AFFILIATION: Pentecostal Assemblies
of Canada

YEAR FOUNDED: 1929

Canada is full of God's activity. Arenas and coffee shops are as common across the country as loons and mosquitoes. In my conversations with church leaders, those who have made significant connections with their communities are usually engaged in both places. These are the common-ground areas where neighbours gather, and the kinds of places you will discover what God is doing.

This is not just the work of the church leader, because going missional is for everyone. For a congregation to become missional, it must re-envision itself and revisit its understanding of leadership and laity.

Too often, people in the pews see God's work as something reserved for the professionals. The job of the clergy is not to bring God to town, because God is already there and at work. Their task is to understand the community, discover what God is doing, and then get on board.

Being missional also transforms congregants from observers to participants—not only in a church program—but participants in the activity of God all around them. School halls, job sites, coffee shops and sports arenas are all places where people can get on board with what God is doing.

Being missional opens the doors of the church so that the people can get out, and the community can get in. Going missional takes church on the road, sometimes literally, to touch people where they are, instead of expecting them to find us where we are.

—W.M.

⋏   ⋏   ⋏

Riding a unicycle down Summit Street in downtown Halifax is no easy task. But that's the challenge Peter Funke, community development pastor at Faith Tabernacle, gave to students at The Halifax Youth Attendance Centre (HYAC), housed upstairs in their church. An unusual challenge for no ordinary classroom. Students who attend the centre—"a one-stop shop for young offenders," according to teacher Tracey Devereaux—are exercising one of their last options for rehabilitation.

The center needed a home before it found its permanent location. Faith Tabernacle opened its doors and welcomed in the 20 or so youth and HYAC staff. "It's not the regular clientele you'll find in a church premise," says Tracey. "I bet this church hasn't heard this kind of language, for example, since its construction days. But the patience of these pastors has been amazing. We've had some challenges, and things happen that wouldn't normally be welcome in a church, but these guys see the big picture."

The day of the unicycle, Peter offered a $50 gift certificate to the student who could learn to ride it the length of the sidewalk in front of the church. "His purpose was simple," says Tracey. "He wanted to give a lesson to these guys to set a goal and realize it takes practice and hard work to reach it." And within two weeks, one of them did.

Faith Tabernacle's senior pastor is John Cheyne, an Irishman who moved from Australia to minister at Faith Tabernacle. He talks sheep when he's talking missional. "In Ireland, when we want to protect sheep, we build a wall and pen the sheep in. But in Australia, because the area is so vast, we dig a well and the sheep will come to the well. We all want to be outward-looking, but it's scary. We become fearful and build a wall to protect ourselves from the world." That has been one of the main missional challenges for Faith Tabernacle—like so many other well-established churches—shifting the centre of gravity to be outward-looking instead of inward-feeding.

Part of digging missional wells in Halifax was to spend time pondering what the gospel looks like in Halifax specifically, and to resist the siren call of the suburbs. John has witnessed a few inner-city Halifax churches relocating to outlying areas for all sorts of reasonable reasons, but that kind of move is not part of the vision for Faith Tabernacle.

"We want to become part of the community we are in. Being missional is more than a program—it's making ourselves available at every level. We're prepared to partner and harvest any opportunities," says John.

One of the more obvious opportunities is the weekly mother's group that meets on Thursday mornings. The church advertises it by placing a sandwich board on the busy sidewalk (beware of unicycles!) outside their front door. Neighbourhood moms, many from low-income households, know it is a safe and welcoming place to gather. Opportunities to pray with the mothers do come up. But more often than not, the Christian message is held lightly and lived out rather than spoken aloud.

The church has been intentional about hosting non-churchy activities and community events. The Halifax Youth Attendance Centre is the most dramatic example, but choral events, orchestras and a Messiah from Scratch, when anyone and everyone can sing along, also opens Faith's doors to the broader community.

"We want to contribute to the moral and physical health of our community, as well as the spiritual," says John. "We don't want to burn down and have no one miss us. We want to contribute and be part of the community."

When Peter Funke first arrived in Halifax from Australia to join the team at Faith Tabernacle, he spent six
months riding Metro Transit buses, sitting in parks and
just talking to people. He wanted to feel Halifax in his
bones and understand the heartbeat of one of Canada's
oldest cities. What was uniquely Halifax about Halifax?
How could Faith Tabernacle be a bright light in this particular place, at this specific time?

"It is not about one size fits all. People think they can
buy a book on missional churches and make it happen.
That is not my experience of how it works," says Peter.
"The Church thinks that being missional is about being
more creative and getting people in the door. And there are
some churches, that I think no matter what you do, would
only see ministry to their own club as a priority. I work between the church and the community. I try and get people
to stop coming to church, and start *being* the church."

And that is not just being the church for the sake of
Faith Tabernacle. Peter's mandate includes building
bridges with other Halifax churches so that, together, they
can build a stronger bridge into the city.

G-ROC, or Go Reach Our City, is a Sunday School on
wheels—as in one very large truck—that visits five
neighbourhoods in the Halifax Regional Municipality (including Dartmouth, literally a bridge away). G-ROC uses
resources and people-power from nine (currently) different
churches who have joined together for this street-ministry
to the city. The program reaches kids from four to 12 years
old and is loud, noisy, messy, hands-on fun presenting the

gospel to children who might not make it to church on a Sunday.

"G-ROC ministries are relationally-based, sidewalk Sunday School that delivers the program to the street, and then visits the families during the week," says Peter.

That means 500 families during the week, each and every week. Sometimes it's just a chat at the door, other times, it's a heart-to-heart in the living room. Volunteers might just share what is happening that week at G-ROC, touch base with the children who attend and encourage them to keep coming, or catch up on what's happening in the mother's workplace.

"When you go into their houses and realize the kids don't have snow suits, or the washing machine is breaking down, and you fix those things, you start earning the right to be heard," says Peter. "It's a long-term thing, developing relationships."

Long-term is key. Peter believes that in some high-need communities, there is a sense of being burnt by a style of church outreach that is dependent on the passion of the person doing the ministry. When that person has used up their enthusiasm, or their schedule changes, the program stops.

Event-based evangelism poses the same kinds of problems. Teams sometimes parachute into Halifax, present an event and have their own feel-good experience. Then they leave.

"We run around and put things on and we put them in our annual reports as outputs, but the question for me is outcomes," says Peter. "Research shows that a very small percentage of people reached by a one-time evangelism event is attending a church after 12 months."

Alternatively, Peter reports that about 30 per cent of people touched by G-ROC are now plugged into churches. "Two years ago, half these kids were using Jesus as a swear word. Now they're coming to G-ROC, and we are visiting their homes."

Training is essential for the 50 or so G-ROC volunteers. Teams have the opportunity to attend Brooklyn Boot Camp, a training program that gives Halifax's street ministers the opportunity to experience inner-city ministry in New York City. The training emphasizes a discovery of what it takes to bring the gospel to your *own* city. The G-ROC program is inspired by Pastor Bill Wilson's work in inner-city outreach to children in New York, using a Sunday School model.

Bringing volunteers onto the same page by sending them for this training has been a major plus for the ministry. "Everybody has their own idea of kids' ministry or women's ministry, or whatever," says Peter. "It's not until you all have a shared experience and see the same thing that unity comes."

G-ROC has also stretched organically into new territory. One day Peter received a call from a mortgage broker with one of those crazy God-ideas. He wanted to form a team of brokers to provide financial assistance to families to help them buy their own homes. The team would donate 50 per cent of the payment they would normally receive when someone refinances a home or buys a mortgage through them. Halifax Christians are encouraged to purchase their mortgages through these particular brokers, to build that very fund.

The fund, called the Halifax Jubilee Corporation, currently hovers around $100,000. The team estimates it would take about $10,000 to make the difference between a typical G-ROC family getting into a house or not. To qualify for housing assistance, the family is required to take a marriage, parenting and finance course to ensure they are on track.

Meanwhile, back inside the four walls of Faith Tabernacle, the teaching, the prayer, the worship and the subsequent shifting of the centre of gravity continues. Curtis Sangster has attended Faith Tabernacle for 17 years. He can feel the movement.

"What I see as missional in our church right now is the way we are getting into the community in ways we haven't before," says Curtis. His own life and work have shifted along with his church. "I had the epiphanal moment about what my purpose is. I went from working for someone in construction to working for myself. I am able to serve through my construction company."

Curtis and his company do pro-bono house repairs for Metro Turning Point, a government-run shelter. "I've learned that my calling is my business. Seeing the need and finding a way to meet it is just powerful to me." Curtis says that there is a culture being cultivated at Faith Tabernacle to be God's hand in the community. "John says to 'get off your rusty dusty and do something!'" he laughs. According to Curtis, Faith Tabernacle was the big thing in the 1960s and 1970s. It was a full house every Sunday. Things have changed. "Since I've been involved, there have been people who have pined for those days. But now, we are more in the community, instead of trying to bring the community in."

SOME OF WHAT THEY LEARNED ALONG THE WAY

- **Customize for your community.** What works in one city, for one church, may not translate into your setting. Take time to get to know your community. Ride the buses, sit on the benches, have those conversations that reveal the needs and desires in front of you. Listen. This may be especially important for congregations, and leadership that has been in a community for a long time. It just might be time to get reacquainted.

- **Work with other churches.** Not every church was interested, and not every board of every church that is now involved was interested at first. But there were often a few passionate parishioners from different churches that wanted to be involved in G-ROC, and that was just the beginning.

- **Open your doors.** From the extreme example of housing a school for delinquent youth, to the more typical mother's drop-in morning, Faith Tabernacle welcomes the community inside its doors.

- **"Pray, but at the same time build the wall (Nehemiah-style),"** says the team at Faith Tabernacle. As you pray for God to show you what to do, realize that you are *already* the answer for which others—before you—have prayed.

- **Find a niche that is not already being filled.** Active Living for Seniors, (ALFS), is another flagship Faith Tabernacle program that, along with other community organizations, provides "exercise, nutrition, medical, social, spiritual and life information opportunities for mature people."

    ALFS has empowered older members of Faith Tabernacle to be missional with their peers in a way that participation in the more active—and loud—G-ROC did not.

    "We want to mobilize our whole community, to reach our whole community," explains John Cheyne.

- **Seek like-minded people.** Find the folks within your church community with both a missional heart and a desire to come on board. Many of the current leadership at Faith Tabernacle did not volunteer for missional service at first. But as these leaders see the missional program take shape and generate lasting fruit (as with G-ROC), the Faith Tabernacle team says that they often become impassioned and join the fray—and often these "converts" become your greatest advocates.

MISSIONAL DISCUSSION

1. Who are the unexpected people from your community that you could welcome into your church facility?

2. How could your church volunteers be better trained so they are "on the same page?"

3. What are your wells? Where are your walls?

THE CHALLENGES OF GOING MISSIONAL

As I called churches across Canada to explain the project we were working on, I encountered a mixed reaction to the word missional. Some churches who are as missional as missional can be don't always use it. They are leery of buzz. They hate to appear to be swept up in what could be, for some people, a fad.

A few people I interviewed asked me to first define exactly what I meant by missional—a question that at first left me scrambling as I struggled to name missional's many faces.

One church told me they prefer words like organic, while others don't actually have a specific label to capture what they are up to in their community. Their missional activity feels more like a natural expression of the trajectory of outward love that their church has been on recently. That seems right.

My interviewees, generous with their time and their stories, usually wanted to know if we were on the same page before we began to really talk. I even had to do some wooing of people reluctant to engage in anything that seemed superficial, that would present being missional as easy and shiny and pre-packaged. I assured them that we really were on an authentic search to try to capture a little of what was happening across Canada as more and more churches tap into the missional movement. We were not after a blueprint. We were after inspiration.

For many, many churches, the word "missional" captures something important and real. It is a word that wraps itself around both an awakening and a remembering of who the Church is, of whose the Church is, and what the Church can be in the world today. It's a word you can bounce around your congregation to see who catches it. It's a word you can run with. A few of us out there need to be reminded every now and then of something as ancient as "love your neighbour."

We are excited about it again. It does feel new. And new does feel good.

"God is always renewing the Church and this is just another round of it," says Cam Roxburgh, director of Forge Missional Training Network, an organization that equips leaders and churches to become missional and transform neighbourhoods across Canada. "My own personal opinion is that 'missional church' is a redundant phrase. You don't need both those words. I don't see an option for the Church."

This round of renewing seems to be targeting our comfort and private satisfaction as consumers of our faith, instead of practitioners.

"You walk into most churches across the country, and what you will see in the service is consumerism," says Cam. "Did you feed me properly? Did you have the right music for me? Is this the coffee I want?" Consumerism is about bringing people in and making us happy when we get there. "We give our people what they want, and that's how they've become consumers. But I don't want to give people what they want. I want to do what's right, not what works," says Cam. "How are we going to help our people move from being consumers to being missionaries again?"

Being missional puts us back out on the streets on purpose, for a much higher purpose. Cam argues that we will begin that transition for real when we learn to ask how we can be faithful. And anyone who has asked that particular question knows that the answer is rarely comfortable. But it's almost always missional. The fact that it's being asked at all, and perhaps increasingly, is good news.

"It's an unbaked cake yet. It's changing the question from 'how do I be successful?'" says Cam.

I asked Cam, who is also pastor of the multi-site Southside Community Church in Surrey, B.C., how a church leader reaches a point where they don't care so much about numbers in the pews, about success in that obvious church-growth kind of way. "It just hurts too much," says Cam. "It comes to a point where an incredible frustration grows inside, and pastors just think 'I can't do this anymore.' Kingdom language is really important now, rather than church growth language."

Of course, not everyone speaks Kingdom, and some of us take longer to become fluent than others, another challenge to a church going missional. John Cheyne, senior pastor of Faith Tabernacle in Halifax, speaks of "five years of really hard slog to get people to reflect back in excitement that we are making ourselves available, not as a single program, but as a church.

"God is pretty earnest about winning the city here," says John. "Sometimes it's the Christians we need to convince. It takes a lot of patience, and it's one step forward and two steps down. It's going home and having to encourage yourself in the Lord, because no one else is encouraging you. And looking for that little green shoot that is starting to grow, because that is God at work."

Going missional is a massive change inside a church, happening at the same time as massive changes are happening in the culture and communities we hope to enter more fully. Navigating through change upon change—against a backdrop of even more change—can be perplexing, even for those of us with the most reliable of compasses.

There are missional thinkers out there, says Cam, who believe that the established Church is too set in its ways to change, and that going missional happens best on a clean slate. Cam himself doesn't agree with that—and this book is testimony to the fact that established churches can turn themselves inside out. But the fact that fresh starts are so appealing testifies to the gritty, long work that is required to turn a church's focus from inward to outward.

As I spoke to church after church, some weeks I felt exhausted just hearing about all the great stuff we could be doing—should be doing. My own response to the activity that is connected with missional hinted at another challenge. Going missional must not turn into the biggest to-do list of all time. Cam pointed out that the best definition of missional touches on faithfulness "in all areas of the Church. It has implications for the way we gather, for all areas of the Church to look at how our actions reflect the nature of the God we believe in."

If missional becomes just about doing stuff, than this would seem like a step backwards into busy. Thinking of going missional as "a renewing of God's people," as Cam defines it, with implications that go beyond even moving from inward to outward, can help us mitigate that risk. Going genuinely missional would seem to go hand in hand with deep prayer and good theology. And we do need theological bearings every step of the way, says John Knight of Main Street Baptist in Saint John.

"It has to proceed from a theological framework. If it doesn't, you run into the danger of volunteering," says John. "Being incarnational is an essential part of being missional and having a kingdom mentality, or you will have people do this as a feel-good exercise, instead of a theologically-fired exercise. It goes back to the fact that you have to be in it for the long-haul. It's an open-ended sense of call from God."

For people who prefer short-hauls with start-and-end dates you can mark on your calendar and defined criteria to measure success, going missional as incarnational and all-encompassing might just challenge everything they have built their experience of Church around. Those who are going missional, one step at a time, say that it is worth the pain and the fuss.

There once was a woman who joined a Bible study I helped lead. I am certain she had never been to a group like ours before. I wondered if she felt as out of place as she seemed to be on the surface. Sometimes, between studies, I'd see her at the grocery store. I almost always tried to avoid her, because I was almost always in a hurry, and she felt like so much work to me.

One week, as I led the study group through some safe discussion of a passage we all had studied before, our visitor made a comment that made me wish I had stayed home with Regis and Kelly, instead of being stuck here, now, in this awkward, outrageous moment.

I wanted to say, "Could you please just sit there quietly?" I felt uncomfortable. I knew she made others uneasy and I was cranky that she was making our calm, easy Thursday mornings so complicated. Even though we were excited when she first showed up—as if her very presence proved how open and welcoming we were—to our unspoken relief, she only came a few times. And the reason I am writing "she" and "the woman" is because at this moment, I can't even remember her name. Being missional demands more from us. And Jesus surely asks more of me.

Beyond the theological and leadership challenges of going missional, for the people in the pews where I sit every
Sunday, missional means that we become owners of the
gospel in a way that we may not have been for a while, if
ever. We have to move ourselves over the hurdle of thinking that we pay clergy the big bucks so they can do the
gospel stuff for us. This can take some time. It might make
some of us leave because we prefer to stay safe.

Missional might mean welcoming people into our lives
that we are not used to. This is a challenge for many of us.
It means we, the comfortable and insulated, have to learn
how to relate, listen deeply and be willing to be transpar-
ent with the fact that we don't actually have it all together
all the time.

It is a missional challenge of no small consequence to
transform from a taker to a giver. It is an even deeper challenge to not fall into the trap of believing that the world is
very lucky indeed that I have finally shown up. And it's a
personal missional challenge to come face to face—as I
have again and again—with what a jerk I can be. My short-
lived commitment to all I say I believe in sends me skedad-
dling back to my comfort zone again and again. Multiply
this by an entire congregation and you can see where the
biggest challenge is—it's in our hearts. Maybe that is
where some of the spiritual growth found in serving actually comes from; sometimes when the light is shining in the
darkness, you can see yourself really, really clearly. Now,
there's a challenge if there ever was one.

"Going missional is messy and intensive. It's a long-
term investment in people's lives. There are tremendous

demands that go with it. You'd better be prepared to deal with that," cautions John Knight.

Many of us aren't ready—yet. But we can be. And we surely will be as we risk to be God's Church instead of our own, forgive ourselves for our weaknesses along the way, and be willing to embark on a joyful, sometimes painful re-imagining of the Church and our part in it as we take one step at a time towards going missional.

⋏   ⋏   ⋏

As the denominational body I belong to determined to become aligned to a missional paradigm, we knew that there would be challenges. Not only does change invite challenge, but the missional church concept itself is defined by challenge. Becoming missional requires you to be comfortable with the unfamiliar and at ease with the unknown.

Missional leaders are committed to messiness. *God is responsive—responsive to need, responsive to open hearts. A missional leader must learn to listen and overhear the voice of God's passion through the people. What is God laying on people's hearts?*

For leaders, this can be messy. It means being able to adjust to where the Spirit is rustling. This can challenge long held programs and threaten pet projects. Leaders who determine that God only communicates through them will almost surely miss what God is saying through the congregation. To be committed to stay aligned with God's activity is a commitment to responsiveness and change—and that means a commitment to messiness.

Missional leaders are committed to mystery. *As attuned as we are to God, we will never fully anticipate the move of God.*

Context is ever changing. Disasters force a new reality, and create a sudden context of need.

God is always aligned to need, so the missional leader must be ready to keep in step with the movement of God. Each day has potential for good and potential for harm. God will engage with both probabilities. The missional leader is at ease with the mystery of each new day—knowing that God knows how to respond to whatever comes along.

Missional leaders are committed to meaning. *Because God is intensely responsive, the activity of God is always relevant. The church that is aligned with God's activity is a church that is relevant and offers meaning. Missional leaders seek to keep in step with God. God is never irrelevant.*

Being committed to messiness, mystery and meaning is not an easy task. It creates a sense of restlessness because the missional leader knows he or she will not always get it right.

My travels with World Vision Canada have given me the opportunity to witness many leaders at work. Leaders helping their church to go missional possess a certain kind of restlessness. Missional leaders are restless knowing they have not yet become—nor ever will be—fully aligned with God's activity.

Yet, in spite of the challenges, there is a deep joy in becoming more aligned to what God is doing. It is not easy. There will be resistance. There will be misunderstanding. There will be work to do. But when you become a part of the impact that God is having, there is great fulfilment.

Recently, the pastor of a church I was visiting turned to me in a worship service and with a beaming smile, declared, "I love Church."

Indeed, the more leaders become aligned with God's activity, the more they will love Church—and the more the Church will reflect God's love.

—W.M.

WHAT I LEARNED ALONG THE WAY

Missional is the newest, oldest thing. Which is probably why it resonates so deeply, moves so profoundly—and truly seems to be changing the landscape of the Canadian Church.

In my experience, we often weave a nourishing cocoon in Church World. It's wonderfully life-giving, and probably necessary—for a time. But then we get stuck in it. We are well-fed, chubby with belonging, but irrelevant. And I suspect we also become really, really bored. Because, of course, cocoons grow dry and tedious. They suffocate us. We were not made for them, and they were not designed for long-term living. We long to bust out.

Going missional is our way out. And as many have said, it's not rocket-science. That's one of the things that makes it so lovely. Being missional is joining in with what God is already doing—and it turns out that, apparently, God is doing quite a bit, everywhere you turn. Being missional means pulling our heads out of our churchy, lint-free belly-buttons and entering into the world we were never called to leave in the first place. God certainly didn't leave it.

To convince the Church—including lazy, busy me—that our experience as Christians is not about receiving a soul massage every Sunday morning is a big, wrenching shift. We are invited to come, so that we can go again. Be, then do. We are not the shut-ins, we are the sent out.

As I researched the churches featured in this book, I spoke to preachers and leaders who, in their current Canadian church and culture context, probably sound as radical in their message as any prophet ever has. They might as well be standing at the foot of a mountain, bedraggled and bothersome to the gawking, thinning crowd.

I am married to a minister. I have sat through many services where I marvelled at my husband Brent's ability to seemingly make an entire church uncomfortable. He is as fearless as I am fearful. The missional message makes people—lazy, busy me again—uncomfortable. Sometimes it makes us want to leave the churches where all that wild and woolly preaching is going on—the kind that kicks us out of the church and back into the world, and head to that other church in the hills where things are safe and predictable. It stinks when people leave churches because they are mad, or threatened, or tired out and confused. It's sad for everyone. Prophetic is rarely pretty.

What I heard, over and over again in the interviews I did for this book (and there were 46 of them) was that the teaching and preaching that leads to a church slowly, painfully, awkwardly, turning itself inside out to face the world once again takes time—and it costs. Churches, especially well-established ones who have had a longer time to grow comfortable and cut-off, do not become missional overnight. But, all across Canada, it is happening.

It took us a long time to grow inward; it will take a while to become outward. There is a tenacity and a boldness that I heard again and again, in the talk that accompanies the missional walk.

Todd Petkau at Riverwood Community Church in Winnipeg tells people that, "if you're coming to this place and heard there's good music and drama, you're taking up a seat that someone else could use. We're not into the show. We're here to help you find your place of serving." He tells them, at least twice a year so they really get it, that the main thing is not the Sunday service, but that they are serving in the community.

Mark Buchanan at New Life Church on Vancouver Island did "years and years of teaching" on servanthood, on racism, on who and what the Church is for and about. Finally, it clicked, sort-of. He's honest to say that this church that probably sounds so deeply missional to the rest of us is also still trying to figure this missional thing out.

For Christ Church, Oshawa, the missional awakening—or maybe it is best to say missional remembering—of the congregation coincided with Judy Paulsen's realization that her own seminary training only 11 years ago focused mostly on caring for the flock. It had not prepared her for a changing Canadian culture. A culture in which the flock is pretty much ignored by the rest of the field. Teaching—

prophetic and patient—is part of the missional picture. And it's happening from coast to coast.

But, of course, it's not all about the pastor. Some of the strongest missional energy and the best ideas rise up from the congregation, as it should. They often come from parishioners with a gift, who see a need. The most creative, missional things happen when someone's passion gets practical. Like Chad Berg in Winkler, Manitoba, the car-guy who, with the support of his pastor and church, created G-Force, providing cars for the car-less, along with a lot of hope and support. Or Rob Thiessen, a parishioner from Coquitlam Alliance who galvanized local church leadership, including his own, to provide shelter for the homeless. He says that he just reminded the churchy people he spoke to what Jesus was about.

Pastors I spoke with were quick to point out that most of the best ideas for missional outreach were not their own, but that their job was to enable when needed, empower when required, equip where necessary—and applaud.

I was very curious as I spoke to churches who were engaging in missional life, to find out if their churches had grown as a result. The answer is, not surprisingly, "yes and no." One pastor laughed. And laughed.

Forest Grove in Saskatoon is a robust church with an average of 800 on Sunday mornings. But pastor Bruce Enns says that attendance seems to have plateaued in recent years. "We have eight pastors on staff here, and when we evaluate all the involvement of everybody during the week, hardly any of it would have resulted in anyone ever showing up on Sunday morning," he says. Bruce, whose church could certainly be described at one point on its journey as attractional, says that, "So often, in North American churches, we have this score card of who shows up on Sunday morning. Being missional means that doesn't matter quite so much. That no longer can be the be-all and end-all of what it means to be the Church."

Sighs of relief can be heard from one corner of the country to another.

As I asked about church growth, I revealed my own split heart. My question felt like a confession that I didn't quite get missional—as if I was implying an ulterior motive on the part of churches that wasn't so missional after all. That's because the ulterior motive part of me—which is alive and well—thinks that missional might just be the most covert church-growth op yet. Surely, the Church serving is the Church appealing? Isn't the most enlightened goatee-sporting pastor among us secretly hoping that if they invite the local Kiwanis to use the hall for free, that Fred will bring the family back on Sunday?

I'm not sure. What I heard was a weariness at the question. Pastors are tired of talking about how many people they can lure in on a Sunday morning. I don't blame them. The people I spoke with seemed genuinely more interested in the church growing in faithfulness. They are interested in their churches and the communities in which they live growing in health and justice—towards Kingdom come—and a realization that, look and see, God is alive and well among you.

Wouldn't it be great for church leaders to no longer feel they have to compare church size when they meet up with the guy who used to sit beside them in Hebrew class? Why couldn't success be measured in terms of the number of times somebody who already does come to church moves out of their comfort zone and into the danger zone of loving their neighbour recklessly, in a God-way?

Tim Plett from The Table in Winnipeg has done Big Church. Now, he does the other kind. "As a ministry professional, I am now at a place where, honestly, I'd rather have the right 50 there." And Nouvelle Vie in Montreal is living proof that the right 50 can—eventually—lead to the right 3,500. But going missional, thankfully, finally, implies that maybe that is not the main point of it all.

When my own home church, in Port Perry, Ont., embarked on an outreach program called the Unextreme Home Makeover (inspired from another church we read about), we worked hard to actually, truly believe that the small home improvement projects we were doing for community members in need were not about luring them into the Church of the Ascension. We talked about it in the group. The new kitchen we put in for a single mother, the walls we painted, the cupboards we emptied and reorganized, were about showing the love of Christ by lending hands that had no strings attached to tie someone into a pew. It was also about us learning to serve.

Which is another theme in each of the stories in this book: the remarkable learning laboratory found in serving. It is almost a cliché in overseas mission trips that those who give, receive, usually more than they leave behind. Apparently, that's also true when you clean up dog doo-doo in

Winnipeg, or do the laundry for a homeless man in St. Catharines and make a lunch for a child in Saint John.

As the Church as a body goes through the beautiful, corporate transformation of local service, so can the individuals carrying it out. Cate, at Southridge Community Church—a congregation that has literally brought the homeless inside—cried for the beauty of it. And listening to her, so did I.

Rick, a Winnipeg policeman who attends Riverwood Community Church, says that doing missional work through his church and hearing the teaching that has come alongside it, "creates a constant awareness of yourself, an accountability within me. It's not just for Sunday, you need to be that every day." For the first time in his Christian life, Rick really, truly feels he's actually living the Christian life. And he's really glad about that.

Fran, at Christ Church in Oshawa, marvels at how that church's outreach and mission committee has grown from writing cheques to being connectors between their church and the community. She senses intuitively that this is the way to go.

Missional makes sense to the church. And it makes sense to the world, which doesn't make us *of* the world, but it can make us a gift to it.

Partnerships were a huge component of many of the missional adventures I learned about. Ask, then listen, says Judy Paulsen of Christ Church, Oshawa. Going out to meet with community groups, asking how the church can serve them, then coming up with creative partnering possibilities seems to be a staple of the missional life.

Intrigued by what I was hearing, I shared this idea with our church's outreach and mission team. They were excited at the thought of creating partnerships with people in the community who weren't necessarily Christian, or the least bit churchy at all. Inspired and energized, we formed a team (me and my friend Joanne) to go visit the local schools and offer our church's assistance for students in need, or... anything really.

We sat across from perplexed school principals who—literally—did not know what to do with the two eager women in their offices. We confessed our own uncertainty of what this thing we were offering would look like. We shared our heart to be a church that cares and that is present, available to the community. Then we left, kind-of embarrassed, a bit deflated, surprisingly giggly, but still certain that we had taken the first important steps down a road that clearly led us straight out of everybody's comfort zones. We will revisit this and voluntarily head back to the principal's office. Understandably, our friends in the community might require a bit of adjustment time if we swoop in too quickly. We'll walk softly for a while.

One of the bonuses of this project was to speak to some of those partners—members of the community in which a missional church lives and breathes, who doesn't necessarily attend that particular church, or any church at all. But they work with them.

"I'm not a big church person but I'm the biggest fan in the world of Main Street Baptist," said Scott Crawford, chair of one of the community groups that Main Street Baptist comes alongside. "They live what they preach. For me, that's a big thing," shared Tracey Devereaux, a teacher in the school for youth hosted by Faith Tabernacle in Halifax. To be perceived as relevant and genuine, to be given the privilege of actually practicing what we preach—and not being preachy as we practice it—must do wonders for God's reputation, a weighty and precious thing we protect.

Years ago, my best friend Janet and I went from Halifax to Vancouver and back again on a student Via-Rail pass. For 21 days of unlimited travel we sat, slept and snickered in coach seats, eating peanut butter sandwiches and once an entire cream pie. We giggled through endless northern Ontario, cackled our way through the stunning prairies, and then, to our utter bewilderment, another passenger finally snapped.

The man, who in my memory is woefully middle-aged and boring, much as I am now, stood up and shouted, "Would you please stop that incessant giggling!" The rest of the car exploded into applause. They weren't clapping for us. Amazingly, they were clapping for the man who told us to shut up.

We were stunned to discover not everyone—not anyone, actually—thought we were the cat's meow. That's how the church is to some people, in some neighbourhoods. Coquitlam Alliance discovered this when they tried to open the doors of their church to the homeless, and had to rezone to do it. Neighbours protested. They painted signs. People shouted, called and complained. The church tapped into an anger and frustration that, in some cases, had less to do with the homeless, and more to do with the holy and where they park their cars on Sunday. The church had the opportunity to introduce themselves and their mission to their neighbours in a new and deeper way. And through endless meetings and countless phone calls, they made friends.

Being missional has quite a bit to do with being a good, fine friend. When I walked through the halls of Southridge Community Church in St. Catharines, chatting with Jeff Lockyer and Tim Arnold about the pluck and passion it takes to stick a homeless shelter right down the hall from your sanctuary, they pointed out something simple and splendid. Genuine friendship is what the Church can bring to the homeless. There are a bunch of government pro-grams out there providing training, health care, even hous-ing. But who will be a friend good enough and long enough to help someone who is homeless believe they are worthy of receiving the help they need? To make sure they make it to their meetings, finish their courses, show up for ap-pointments, get that cut on the leg taken care of? And even give them nice pyjamas to sleep in, because why in the world wouldn't we do that simple, gracious thing?

That is what the Church can do, sometimes brilliantly. Of course, there are lots of other people who care about the homeless and the hurting in the world. Jeff knows that well. He partners with them every day. But what we bring, and what churches all across Canada—of all shapes, sizes and denominations—are increasingly bringing to their communities, is Christ himself. And to our humility and joy, discovering that He is already there.

ABOUT THE AUTHORS

Karen Stiller is an award-winning freelance writer and associate editor of *Faith Today* magazine. She writes for a variety of North-American publications and non-profit organizations, with a focus on social justice issues. Karen and her husband Brent Stiller, a minister, have three children and they live in Port Perry, Ont.

Willard Metzger is Director of Church Relations for World Vision Canada (WVC). Willard engages with churches and denominations across the country to create awareness about global poverty issues and help churches partner with WVC projects overseas, while providing church leaders with tools to mobilize their congregations for justice and compassion. Willard has decades of experience as a pastor, lecturer and missions specialist. He and his wife Lois live in Drayton, Ont. They have two grown children.